The Great Deception of the Mandela Effect

The Great Deception of the Mandela Effect

The Great Deception of the Mandela Effect

by
Lewis Stanek

The Great Deception of the Mandela Effect

All scripture quotations, unless otherwise noted, are taken from the King James Version of the bible.

This book may contain copyrighted material the use of which has not always been specifically authorized by the copyright owner. We are making such material available in an effort to advance understanding of environmental, political, human rights, economic, democracy, scientific, and social justice issues, etc. we believe this constitutes a 'fair use' of any such copyrighted material as provided for in section 107 of the US Copyright Law.

Copyright © 2017 by Lewis Stanek
All rights reserved. This book or any portion thereof may not be reproduced or used in any manner whatsoever without the express written permission of the publisher except for the use of brief quotations in a book review or scholarly journal.

First Printing: 2017

ISBN-13: 978-1545573655

ISBN-10: 1545573654

The Great Deception of the Mandela Effect

Dedicated to all those who I have known and loved throughout the years of my life. You know who you are.

The Great Deception of the Mandela Effect

The Great Deception of the Mandela Effect

Contents

Preface	9
Introduction	11
Chapter One	17
Chapter Two	27
Chapter Three	33
Chapter Four	43
Chapter Five	92
Chapter Six	102
Chapter Seven	118
Chapter Eight	146
Chapter Nine	154
Appendix A	162
Appendix B	166

The Great Deception of the Mandela Effect

The Great Deception of the Mandela Effect

Preface

I can't help but believe that the Mandela effect is an important subject to discuss even though many people laugh it off as a simple matter of poor memory among a large portion of the planet's population, Nothing more than an epidemic of confabulation. I personally believe Mandela effects are real changes in ones history and not an instance of something mis-remembered, although mis-memories can and frequently do occur. Some people call it the Mandela Effect, others the quantum effect. Some people believe that it is a matter of the multiverse collapsing in on itself forcing individual realities to merge into one, some suspect the scientists at CERN are attempting to act out a Lovecraftian scheme to open a portal to another dimension to allow the imprisoned fallen angels access to the earth once again. Still, others suggest that those who are experiencing this effect have died in some great cataclysm and were instantly transported to the next closest reality to their own, others wonder if this is a matter of the government experimenting in mass hypnosis. If it is a matter of the governments attempting to impose its own mind control over the

The Great Deception of the Mandela Effect

populace, is it being done by subliminal messages broadcast through television programs, or on the world wide web? Some consider it to be a matter of quantum entanglement. Or is it more of a matter of a spiritual nature? Looking at the many recorded differences in memory, none are clearer in my mind than those differences found in the bible.

Many people attempt to prove their memories are correct by searching for what they call residual evidence. This can be photographic evidence or physical evidence showing history or a text as they remember it to have been. I intend to include an appendix containing some of the photographic evidence found floating around in cyberspace. I will also include a brief appendix of possible verses changed or mis-remembered that I neglected to include in the main body of this book.

The Great Deception of the Mandela Effect

Introduction

What exactly are we discussing when we talk about the Mandella Effect? I am sure many people have never heard of it, or if they have they have discounted it as some sort of urban legend or perhaps early symptoms of Alzheimer's disease. Many, perhaps as many as half the population have experienced this admittedly bizarre effect while others live their life totally unaware of the changes perceived by others going on around them. The term "Mandella Effect" was coined by Fiona Broome to label instances of great numbers of people apparently misremembering settled events of history. She coined the term Mandella Effect, as the story goes, for the reason that very many people will swear that they remember Nelson Mandella dying in prison in the 1990's and not living to become the president of South Africa. Obviously many if not most people remember and accept Nelson Mandella as a major character in world history and know that he lived to

The Great Deception of the Mandela Effect

become President and along with F. W. De Klerk brought an end to apartheid. But, what is the Mandela Effect? Whatis.com defines it as "The Mandela effect is the observed phenomenon of people having clear memories of events that did not occur or misremembering significant events and facts." Snopes defines it succinctly as "The Mandela Effect is a collective misremembering of a fact or event.". Certainly clear and concise, but does that really explain what is being experienced by possibly millions if not billions of people around the world?

The term Mandela Effect was coined in reference to events that large numbers of people around the world share false memories of but is often generalized to refer to any incident of a false memory. The shared mis-memory of Nelson Mandela's death is certainly is one reason to name this effect in his honor, but there is a deeper more descriptive more accurate reason for the name as well.

A circular geometric pattern considered to be a spiritual symbol for the universe in many eastern religions that symbolizes the cosmos metaphysically and is considered as the microcosm of the macrocosm of the universe is called a

The Great Deception of the Mandela Effect

mandala. Mandalas depict radial balance. Meditating on the intricate patterns within the image of a mandala may well be a practice designed to increase one's spiritual unity with the universe. Consider for a moment a circle within a circle within another circle composed of multiple overlapping Earths, Each earth similar yet different from the one before it and the one that comes after. In this sense, the term Mandella may well be better than any other in describing the disorienting effect of suddenly realizing that something you grew up with and have firm memories of never in fact existed, yet something else, perhaps something similar is there in its place. Something, those around you firmly believe has always been there just as it is and always was. Most of the examples frequently mentioned when the Mandella Effect comes up in conversation are matters of trivia. For an example did the character Darth Vader tell Luke Skywalker "Luke, I am your father" or did he say "No, I am your father." If you remember Darth Vader saying "Luke, I am your father" you are experiencing the Mandela Effect. Is it JIF, JIFF, or Jiffy peanut butter? If you remember eating JIFF or Jiffy peanut butter you are

The Great Deception of the Mandela Effect

experiencing the Mandella Effect. Many of the memories are of corporate logos. I have noticed changes in corporate logos many times over the years. I assumed the company was trying something new, perhaps a new cooler hip marketing campaign was in the works. In any event, I wouldn't spend another moment considering the change, but I was missing something.

Imagine Volkswagen didn't always have the space separating the V and the W in their emblem or that Ford didn't always have the little curlicue squiggle in the Capital F of FORD in their emblem. I have owned a couple of Volkswagon beetles and many Fords over the years. I loved the beetles and mourned their passing to the great junkyard in the sky. I tell you truthfully the emblem on the hood of my beetles did not have a break between the capital v and the capital w. The Fords I owned served me well and I swear not one of them had that pigtail squiggle in the capital F of Ford, but now if I go and find one of the same make and year there will be the silly little squiggle as if it had been there all along. I remember eating Fruit Loops as a kid and buying them for my own children, but it apparently never

The Great Deception of the Mandela Effect

was Fruit Loops. It has always been Froot Loops. Was the Department store JC Penny as I remember it or has it always been JC Penney? Was the candy bar Kit-Kat or Kitkat? Warner Brothers Cartoons are Looney Toons or are they Looney Tunes? How about the little rich guy on the Monopoly game box, does he wear a monocle or not? When I first heard of the Mandella effect I thought it was interesting and perhaps would provide me with a little intellectual fun exploring this new urban legend while idly passing the time away. I thought that this was most likely only a matter of a few people suffering from faulty memories. Still, a nice little oddity to contemplate. Nothing of any real importance was effected. Let's face it other than Mandella's death most of the changes mentioned so far are of no consequence to anyone. So for fun, I delved a little deeper, not willing to waste too much time on brand names. To be honest that isn't something I ever paid much attention. I buy generic whenever I have the option, so whether it is Fruit Loops or Froot Loops is no skin off my nose one way or the other.

The Great Deception of the Mandela Effect

The Great Deception of the Mandela Effect

Chapter One

*T*he Mandela Effect includes much from popular culture. Lines from famous movies appear to have changed for some, yet have always been the way they are to others. A few examples from popular films include Star Wars epic series. Did Darth Vader say "Luke, I am your father", or did he say "No, I am your father." I remember "Luke, I am your father", but the line in the movie is now and apparently always has been "No, I am your father". In the film Field of Dreams Did the voice in the cornfield whisper "If you build it they will come." or did it whisper "If you build it he will come."? How about Forest Gump? Did he say "My mother always said life is like a box of chocolates, you never know what you will get." or did she say "Life was like a box of chocolates, you never know what you will get."? The current history tells us it was "Life was like a box of chocolates"

The Great Deception of the Mandela Effect

Although there is residual evidence indicating that at one time it was the other. In the classic Disney feature animation "Snow White" what little incantation does the wicked stepmother recite to the magic mirror? Is it "Mirror, mirror on the wall who is the fairest of them all?" or is it "Magic mirror on the wall who is the fairest of them all?"? If you remember "Mirror, mirror on the wall, you are experiencing the Mandela effect.   Another classic film that shows apparent changes to those of us experiencing the Mandela Effect is The Wizard of Oz. I can't say for sure if there are any changes in the dialog or not, but I am quite sure that when I watched the movie as a child and with my children as they were growing up the scarecrow did not carry a piece, but now if you choose to watch the film you will see the scarecrow waving a silver revolver around while Dorothy, the Cowardly Lion, the Tin woodsman, and the Scarecrow are starting off on their mission for the wizard. For some reason seeing the Scarecrow waving a gun around affected me more than all of the changes in dialog in the other movies mentioned so far. I am sure that there are other apparent changes and mistaken memories related to popular media,

The Great Deception of the Mandela Effect

but I am sure you get the idea. One thing I think may be important to point out is that these mistaken memories or changes appear to be fluid. That is they are not set in stone, not only that, but not everyone who experiences the Mandella Effect shares the same memories. Some remember JIFF peanut butter, some remember Jiffy peanut butter. It is as if we have not all started from the same point or traveled the same road to find ourselves here.

Deaths of the rich and famous is another area where people have differing memories. Of course, I already mentioned the death of Nelson Mandela, but there are differing memories regarding the assassination of President John F. Kennedy. I am sure those of us who were alive when he was shot remember exactly where we were and what we were doing on that fateful day on November 22nd, 1963. I was home sick from school and watched it happen on television. As far as I know no one disagrees regarding his dying on that date, but there is confusion and mistaken memories regarding the car he was riding in and how many passengers were in the car. This would be a good point to bring up residual evidence. Residual evidence in regards to the Mandella

The Great Deception of the Mandela Effect

effect is evidence supporting the memories of those who remember a history other than the one that is currently agreed upon by the majority. The assassination of JFK is a prime example of such evidence. The question isn't whether or not he was murdered on that date, but the type of car he was in and the number of riders. Was it a convertible with front and back seat or a custom stretch convertible with front, middle and back seats. Were there six people in the car or only four? There are photographs from that date, showing both! The official history says he was riding in a stretch convertible and there are photographs to prove it, however, there are also photographs of JFK riding in a convertible with only the standard front and back seats! There is a museum display with wax statues of President Kennedy and the First Lady riding in the convertible with front and back seat only. Finally, Life magazine published a full page photograph of the car he was riding with roses in the back seat as a memorial with the car as a standard convertible with only front and back seats. When considering all of the conspiracy theories regarding John F. Kennedy's murder I wouldn't be surprised if any or all of these photographs have

The Great Deception of the Mandela Effect

been faked, but that in and of itself does not discount the potential presence of the Mandela Effect regarding this event either.

I've mentioned apparent changes in history to company logos, changes in movie dialog and scenes, misremembered details in the deaths of two very famous men all possibly symptoms of the Mandela Effect. World geography is one change that I cannot ignore. I lay no claim to being an expert in geography, far from it, but I do rely on maps when traveling and am familiar with the globe to some extent. That is why I was startled to see South America so far east and so close to Africa and Sicily now looks to be a soccer ball about to be kicked by the boot of Italy. The north pole is now underwater! I clearly remember reading and seeing photographs of the arctic circle being frozen solid, seeing documentaries of Robert Peary and his team traveling by dog sled searching for and finding the north pole, and reading about nuclear submarines patrolling under the ice cap of the north pole, now I come to find that What I thought I knew was the Arctic circle is no longer a habitable frozen mass of ice covering the magnetic north pole is now a

The Great Deception of the Mandela Effect

sometimes frozen sometimes thawed arctic ocean. This is all little more than a tad disturbing. How can continents change position and conditions so quickly and without half or the world's population noticing? The answer, of course, is they can't they have always been the way they are, but that begs the question why do so many of us remember the continents positioned otherwise?

The north pole was a massive 6km thick icecap no ice breaking ships could ever cross that passage, but nuclear powered submarines would travel beneath the North Pole to sneak up on their cold war foes. The Norwegian archipelago of Svalbard did not exist.
South America was 1500km to the west, much further from Africa than it is now. Africa was at least 30% smaller. Greenland was at least 50% smaller. Northern Canada is now appears scattered, not the solid landmass I remember. I suppose all the water from the north pole had to go somewhere when it melted. The Mediterranean Sea was much wider, the gap between Europe and Africa seems ridiculous small now. Several new islands have appeared in the Mediterranean Sea alongside Malta having shifted

The Great Deception of the Mandela Effect

1500km to the west closer to Italy. There are dozens of new islands in the Mediterranean Sea from Greece to Sicily. Australia looks to have moved 1500km up north. No longer as 'down under' as it once was. the Earth is not as many of us remember it.

It is not just a matter of global geography, but also astronomical positioning as well. You may ask, what exactly do I mean by that? The first thing I noticed was that somehow the sun appeared different to me. It appeared both brighter and a different shade of yellow. The sun I recall was a warmer shade of yellow. The sun I see in the sky now is less yellow and more white, almost entirely white. While it has never been advisable to look directly into the sun, in the past one would be able to give it a quick little glance without any harm being done, now the sun is far too bright for even that quick little glance. Also, I remember the sun rising in the east and setting in the west, not rising in the south-east and setting in the southwest as it does now. I mentioned this to my wife, and she acted as if I had lost my mind, not that she thought I presented a danger to myself and or others as she didn't take to the nearest asylum, but as if I was

The Great Deception of the Mandela Effect

becoming just a little too eccentric for my own good. She humored me. I am glad to say that I am not the only one to have noticed this change. Inuit Elders have noted a change in the position of the sun in the sky, they state that global warming is due to a shift in the Earth. They state that the earth has shifted or "wobbled". "Their sky has changed!" The elders declare that the sun rises at a different position now, not where it used to previously. They also state the moon and the stars are not positioned in the sky as they used to be. More details can be found on the web in an article published in nativespress.com.

So there may have been a little wobble in the Earth causing some minor changes in the apparent position of the sun, moon and stars in the sky, nothing too odd, too Mandela about that is there? Well, that isn't the end of it. Do you remember where your teachers taught you the Earth is located in the Milky Way? If you are like me you remember it is somewhere along the edge of the galaxy, but are not able to remember the precise location. Fortunately, there are scientists and astronomers that do remember where the Earth was located and can tell which arm of the galaxy. Neil

The Great Deception of the Mandela Effect

deGrasse Tyson is captured on video stating his location including our position in the galaxy in the Sagittarius arm of the Milky way spiral, as can be seen in this youtube link https://www.youtube.com/watch?v=k-0mLH6rx78 The problem is that in this "reality" the earth is located in the Orion arm of the galaxy positioned much closer to the center of the milky way. We are talking about a difference of thousands if not millions of light years from the remembered position on the Sagittarius arm! Some would have us believe our consciousness has been transported in the twinkling of an eye across the galaxy to a different yet parallel world. Who knows? Who is to say?

    One other item I wish to mention before I forget are Mandela animals. These are described as animals that either were extinct and are now back or animals we never heard of or imagined in our past experience. I find this category of Mandela Effects interesting, but I was never all that good in biology, so I'm not surprised that there are many creatures running around that I never knew existed. I find some truly frightening such as the fox bat! That isn't it's technical name but I'm sure it is the common name it known by. Imagine a

The Great Deception of the Mandela Effect

bat about the size of an eagle with a foxes head that flies around during the day, or the vampire deer, personally I would call it a saber tooth deer. Speaking of fanged creations there is also a fanged squirrel. A large bird that some call a Mandela animal is the shoebill stork, I have never seen one in person, but I did see a photograph where a park ranger is feeding one a fish and the bird is only a little shorter than the ranger. Although I was not aware of any of these animals prior to someone bringing them up as proof of the Mandela effect that in and of itself does not qualify them as signs of the Mandela effect, but who am I to disqualify someone else's experience from my own ignorance.

The Great Deception of the Mandela Effect

Chapter Two

*S*o what are we to make of all of this? There are many different theories being tossed around, but it appears to me that truly no one knows. We each just make our best guess. Of course, there are those who are not experiencing the Mandella effect at all and they tend to think it is all just a matter of some people misremembering things. I suppose they look on it as an early form of dementia. Many people believe they can trace it all back to experiments being conducted at CERN. They suspect that CERN is trying to open a portal into a parallel world and that with each experiment another string of Mandella Effects occurs affecting only certain people. Still, others think it is due to time travel, someone is going back in time to change history for some major event and in the process, a ripple effect changes all sorts of little unrelated things such as brand

The Great Deception of the Mandela Effect

names, or lines in movies. I read a post from one person who suspects that we all died in 2012 and have merged into a parallel world where the disaster did not take place. On a similar note I read the opinion of another person who suspects that since as far as he knows most of the people effect by this are American, that the United States has been nuked and utterly obliterated and again we who experience memories of alternate histories are all dead and have migrated to another more peaceful world and are trying to cope with the changes. I have to admit the thought of mass hypnosis has crossed my mind, but for what purpose? Why would anyone go through the trouble of arranging subliminal messages throughout all the media to give people false memories? Think of the expense and what would be gained? I have heard the theory that we are all trapped in a virtual reality program, a hologram of sorts. I don't accept that we are a group of artificially intelligent characters in a virtual reality video game. I suppose it is possible, but I personally don't like the thought so I focus on other options. I have also had the disturbing thought that perhaps the Mandela effect is not happening at all and this is just a dream or fantasy that

The Great Deception of the Mandela Effect

my brain has cooked up to keep itself entertained while I rot in a coma locked away in some nursing home somewhere, similar to the fate of the lead character in "Johnny got his gun". I have also thought that perhaps we naturally pass from one parallel world to another from time to time without ever noticing the change until recently.

At least one gentleman has posted onto Youtube videos supposed taken from security cameras where people, cars, and animals simply appear out of nowhere. Some examples in the video, in my opinion, have been faked. Those examples that are accompanied by a flash of light appear fake to me, but those where the person or animal simply appears to fade and then disappear ring true to me. Why you may ask, would I accept one and not the other? Simply because I have witnessed the one and not the other. While driving west on a clear summer day I spotted a flock of sparrows ahead of me above the road. First, they as a flock flew north then turned and flew south. They did this a few times. In the process, they began to fade becoming transparent and then they were gone. The oddest thing was that in the back of my mind something was trying to justify

The Great Deception of the Mandela Effect

what I was witnessing, something was trying to keep me calm, to keep me asleep, by reassuring me that this was all normal and that this was how it always happens. At the same time, I wondered if I had suddenly developed a brain tumor, or was having a stroke. I didn't swerve or drive off of the road or have an accident of any kind and after thinking it over decided I must have seen a mirage. Now, after becoming aware of the Madella Effect I suspect that what I witnessed was not a mirage at all.

Perhaps you are familiar with the term maya. In Hinduism and Buddhism maya is the term used to describe the supernatural power by which the universe becomes manifest; the illusion or appearance of the phenomenal world. In other words maya is the physical world in contrast to the spiritual world. The key word in this sentence is illusion. The physical world is believed to be nothing more than maya, illusion, nothing more than a dream. If they are correct, as I believe they may be, what is there to prevent changes in the dream from happening at the whim of the dreamer. I believe that what may be new is not the fact that changes are occurring around us, but the number of people who are

The Great Deception of the Mandela Effect

waking up and are aware of the changes occurring in the world.

I am Christian and and as such do not exactly accept the concept of maya, but I do believe that the spiritual is more real than the physical, and that matter follows spirit. As the bible states in John 1:1-3 In the beginning was the Word, and the Word was with God, and the Word was God. The same was in the beginning with God. All things were made through him; and without him was not anything made that hath been made.

The Great Deception of the Mandela Effect

The Great Deception of the Mandela Effect

Chapter Three

I found the mis-memories and changes mentioned so far in this little book interesting, possibly a good topic for conversation with the right people, but let's face facts a lot of people will just stare at you as if you lost your mind if you bring the subject up and share of few of the apparent changes with them. Other's eyes will brighten and share changes they themselves have noticed. There are those who are awake, those who are waking up, and those who are asleep and would prefer to stay asleep a little longer if you don't mind. That is all fine and good as far as I'm concerned, but when you consider the bible this changes.
Some of the bible is history, some of the bible is poetry, some of the bible is prophecy, The bible contains facts and it contains metaphors, some people take the bible literally, I take the bible seriously. So when it comes to my attention

The Great Deception of the Mandela Effect

that the bible has changed I find that disturbing. When I say changed I don't mean changes made by one group or another to make the bible more politically correct, or more palatable to one special interest group or another such as an Ebonics bible, or a feminist, or LGBT bible. Those are each designed for a specific target audience and contain changes with an agenda supporting those same specific audiences. The changes I'm referring to are changes appearing in the King James bible of 1611. The King James bible is not the only version to be affected by Mandela changes, one can find many of the same changes in any of the other translations or for that matter in documents in the original languages. As in all other Mandela Effect changes noticed, the difference is in the eye or more precisely in the memory of the beholder. Those unaware of the change will rightfully state that what is in the bible was always in the bible and no change has been made.

When I first took it upon myself to begin this project, I had hoped to eventually compile a complete Mandela Effect study bible highlighting all of the changes and referencing the 'original text' as remembered by those that are aware of

The Great Deception of the Mandela Effect

the changes having been made, but I understand that this would be a gargantuan task and perhaps never end as well as it is surely possible that the changes we witness in the text now may not be the only changes. There may be more to come. From my limited understanding, at this point in time, the more bizarre changes appear to be contained in the old testament, such as the word womb being replaced with the word matrix and Holy One being replaced with the holy thing, not to mention Holy God being replaced with holy gods in the book of Daniel.

I personally find the addition of mythical beasts to the bible offensive, but offensive or not, you can now find unicorns where I recall oxen in the bible, not to mention cockatrices, dragons, unicorns, and satyrs. On one site I saw the phoenix bird included on the list, but I could not confirm this in the bible. The bible passages I recall do not include any of these mythical creatures. I do remember Leviathan and Behemoth being mentioned in the book of Job. Leviathan as described sounds like a gigantic creature of the sea that at one time existed, but has now been long extinct. Behemoth as described sounds like a very large land animal perhaps a

The Great Deception of the Mandela Effect

mastodon or something similar, again a creature that may have very well roamed the earth at one time long ago, but now is extinct. However, a cockatrice is a legendary monster, half-rooster, and half-snake, with the ability to turn people to stone at a glance. cockatrices have never been anything but the fanciful mythical creatures of fables. Unicorns, and satyrs also are creatures of legend and myth and have never existed and as I may have stated earlier were not included in the bible I studied. They appear to me to be fanciful additions designed to bring doubt and skepticism to the reader's mind and hamper and discredit their faith in the scriptures. As you will see as you continue reading there have been many apparent changes to the bible, some may appear to be silly, but others diabolical such as the passage in Luke where Christ commands that those who will not obey him be slain. That is most certainly a passage that is totally foreign and out of character for our Lord and I suspect it is a passage that was added to the text just as the other Mandella effect changes were made.

As intriguing as I personally find the Mandella Effect changes in the old testament I believe I should begin with

The Great Deception of the Mandela Effect

the Gospels as I am convinced they contain the essential message of the Bible. I intend to use a public domain version of the 1611 King James Bible for all of the scriptures quoted. I have selected the King James version because I am aware that at this time some of the Mandella effect changes appear to be limited to the King James version while others have spread through to all translations. I suspect that with time all translations may come to contain the same changes and or errors.

One example that comes to mind is the parable of the wineskins. I am sure many of you will remember the parable where Christ talking replying to a question about the fasting in Mathew 9:17 says "Neither do men put new wine into old wineskins: else the wineskins burst and the wine runneth out, and the wineskins perish: but they put new wine into fresh wineskins, and both are preserved." At least that is how I remember the passage. Considering new wine will ferment in the wineskins and a new wineskin will stretch to accommodate the expanding gases where an old wineskin has already been stretched to it's fullest and will simply burst asunder the passage makes perfect sense, both literally

The Great Deception of the Mandela Effect

and spiritually. However the passage, now states "Neither do men put new wine into old bottles: else the bottles break, and the wine runneth out, and the bottles perish: but they put new wine into new bottles, and both are preserved." You might say wineskins, bottles who cares? True this may be a small change yet it works to bring doubt into the reader's mind. In King James and some other versions, this has been changed to bottles whereas in still others such as the New Jerusalem Bible it remains unchanged. This parable makes perfect sense when the word wineskins are used as new wineskins will stretch as the wine ferments and old wineskins will simply burst asunder. Bottles on the other hand although they may break and be more fragile than wineskins they have been reused from their first invention and anyone who has made wine knows when you are letting wine ferment you allow the pressure to be released from a bottle and more likely than that wine would be fermented in a wooden keg and not a bottle at all. Although bottles were first used in Asia around 100 BC and were introduced to Rome in 1 AD and it is possible that bottles could have been used it is unlikely. If a container other than a wineskin was to be used

The Great Deception of the Mandela Effect

in Christ's time it would more likely be a clay jar, not a bottle.

While considering the Mandela Effect on the King James bible a few unchanged bible verses came to mind. I am aware of the irony in using bible verses as a preface to a section regarding changes within the bible itself. However, it is what it is and we make do with what we have. First of all Revelation 22:18-21 warns the reader not to change the text of Revelation. Many have assumed this warning applies to the entire bible, while in fact it applies only to Revelation. Even so I am unwilling to make any changes other than highlighting those verses that appear to have changed from what I remember from my studies and changes others have noticed.

Revelation 22:18-21 "For I testify unto every man that heareth the words of the prophecy of this book, If any man shall add unto these things, God shall add unto him the plagues that are written in this book: And if any man shall take away from the words of the book of this prophecy, God

The Great Deception of the Mandela Effect

shall take away his part out of the book of life, and out of the holy city, and from the things which are written in this book. He which testifieth these things saith, Surely I come quickly. Amen. Even so, come, Lord Jesus. The grace of our Lord Jesus Christ is with you all. Amen."

Matthew 24:24 warns us that in the last days there will be false Christs who if they could would even deceive the elect. Who are the elect? You may ask. Simply put, the "elect of God" are those whom God has predestined to salvation. The elect are the saved believers in Jesus Christ who bear the mark of the Holy Spirit! What I hold dear in this passage is the implied promise that it is impossible to deceive the elect.

Matthew 24:24 "For there shall arise false Christs, and false prophets, and shall shew great signs and wonders; insomuch that, if it were possible, they shall deceive the very elect."

Ephesians 1:13 confirms for us that our salvation is secure as we are sealed with the Holy Spirit.

The Great Deception of the Mandela Effect

Ephesians 1:13 "In whom ye also trusted, after that, ye heard the word of truth, the gospel of your salvation: in whom also after that ye believed, ye were sealed with that holy Spirit of promise, "

Finally 1 Corinthians 2:13 reminds us that the Holy Spirit is our teacher.

1 Corinthians 2:13 "Which things also we speak, not in the words which man's wisdom teacheth, but which the Holy Ghost teacheth; comparing spiritual things with spiritual."

Finally John 14:26 Where Christ promises us that the Father will send the Holy Spirit to teach us all things, and bring all things to your remembrance, whatsoever Christ has taught us. This is where I believe we can hope that we will not be deceived and that we can trust in the promptings of the Holy Spirit in guiding us in understanding our bibles.

John 14:26 "But the Comforter, which is the Holy Ghost, whom the Father will send in my name, he shall teach you

The Great Deception of the Mandela Effect

all things, and bring all things to your remembrance, whatsoever I have said unto you. Peace I leave with you, my peace I give unto you: not as the world giveth, give I unto you. Let not your heart be troubled, neither let it be afraid."

What do I get from those passages? Very simply we who have been marked by the Holy Spirit and belong to Christ have been purchased at a great price and can rely on the Holy Spirit to direct us and guide us in these times of great deception.

The Great Deception of the Mandela Effect

Chapter Four

Matthew 5:17-20 'Do not think that I have come to abolish the law or the prophets; I have come not to abolish but to fulfill. For truly I tell you, until heaven and earth pass away, not one letter, not one stroke of a letter, will pass from the law until all is accomplished. I highlighted until heaven and earth pass away, not one letter, not one stroke of a letter, to help make the following point. Earlier in chapter one, I shared apparent changes in the Earth's geography, apparent changes in the position of the earth in relation to the sun, which was confirmed by Inuit Elders noting a change in the position of the sun in the sky, due to a shift in the Earth. I also shared that there is an apparent change in the Earth's position in the Milky Way. Furthermore, Isaiah 65:17 states 'For, behold, I create new heavens and a new earth: and the former shall not be remembered, nor come into mind. A case can be made that the first Earth and Heavens have passed

The Great Deception of the Mandela Effect

away and have been replaced with new heavens and Earth and there are those who do not remember what was, only what is, while there are those who remember some facts from the old heavens and Earth before the Mandela effect changes took place.

2 Timothy 3:1-17

You must understand this, that in the last days distressing times will come. For people will be lovers of themselves, lovers of money, boasters, arrogant, abusive, disobedient to their parents, ungrateful, unholy, inhuman, implacable, slanderers, profligates, brutes, haters of good, treacherous, reckless, swollen with conceit, lovers of pleasure rather than lovers of God, holding to the outward form of godliness but denying its power. Avoid them! For among them are those who make their way into households and captivate silly women, overwhelmed by their sins and swayed by all kinds of desires, who are always being instructed and can never arrive at a knowledge of the truth. As Jannes and Jambres opposed Moses, so these people, of corrupt mind and counterfeit faith, also oppose the truth. But they will not

The Great Deception of the Mandela Effect

make much progress, because, as in the case of those two men, their folly will become plain to everyone. Now you have observed my teaching, my conduct, my aim in life, my faith, my patience, my love, my steadfastness, my persecutions and suffering the things that happened to me in Antioch, Iconium, and Lystra. What persecutions I endured! Yet the Lord rescued me from all of them. Indeed, all who want to live a godly life in Christ Jesus will be persecuted. But wicked people and impostors will go from bad to worse, deceiving others and being deceived. But as for you, continue in what you have learned and firmly believed, knowing from whom you learned it, and how from childhood you have known the sacred writings that are able to instruct you for salvation through faith in Christ Jesus. All scripture is inspired by God and is useful for teaching, for reproof, for correction, and for training in righteousness, so that everyone who belongs to God may be proficient, equipped for every good work.

   Following is a list of questionable verses. I have highlighted and italicized the questionable word or phrase within the text and may have commented following the

The Great Deception of the Mandela Effect

verse. At least one of the verses listed I personally remember just as it is, yet others don't so I have included it for your consideration. Please realize this is not a comprehensive list of all of the changes. I suspect such a list is not possible as changes may continue to be made even as I write this. I do hope that you, dear reader will take this as food for thought and after prayer requesting the Holy Spirit guide you, explore the bible for yourself. following is an incomplete least of Mandella effect changes found in the King James bible.

Genesis 1:1 In the beginning God created the heaven and the earth. I recall this passage as heavens not heaven, which then goes along with the tradition of three heavens. First, The first is the atmosphere above us. The second heaven is the stellar heaven, the sun, moon, and stars. The third heaven is where God resides, above the other two regions. Or as stated in Wikipedia; "Heaven is therefore spoken of in rather different senses: as another dimension, as the physical skies or upper cosmos, as the realm of divine perfection already in existence, or as the "coming world" at the return of Christ."

The Great Deception of the Mandela Effect

Finally heaven can be understood as the presence of God. However one looks at it though there is more than a single heaven and the change in genesis 1:1 is in error.

Genesis 3:15 Enters an error into scripture of a more devious sort directly attacking the first biblical promise of the coming Christ who would defeat Satan. Genesis 3:15 currently reads "And I will put enmity between thee and the woman, and between thy seed and her seed; it shall bruise thy head, and thou shalt bruise his heel. Does this seem a little off to you? Originally it read "He shall crush thy head". The mandella effect has changed it to " it shall bruise thy head" So the personal God He is transformed into an impersonal it and the fatal blow of crushing Satan's head is changed to a minor inconvenience, a bruise. So it can bee seen from this one example that there is the beginnings of a trend in many of the Mandella changes affected in the King James Bible always leaning towards the negative, always minimizing what is said about the divine and strengthening what is said about the satanic.

The Great Deception of the Mandela Effect

Some of the changes though are or at least appear to be inconsequential such as Genesis 31:37 where the word stuff is added to the passage. Genesis 31:37 "Whereas thou hast searched all my stuff, what hast thou found of all thy household stuff? set it here before my brethren and thy brethren, that they may judge betwixt us both." Genesis 45:20 also includes the word stuff. Genesis 45:20 "Also regard not your stuff; for the good of all the land of Egypt is your's." On face value these both are minor changes that account to little, but it is possible that in the original languages these changes have devious implications.

The word couch has been added to the text replacing bed in Genesis 49:4 "Unstable as water, thou shalt not excel; because thou wentest up to thy father's bed; then defiledst thou it: he went up to my couch." I looked through several different translations of the bible to compare this verse and all of them used the word couch. You may rightly ask; so what? who cares? couch or bed does it really matter? In English probably not, but I would like to point out that The couch was invented by Jay Wellingdon Couch in 1895 therefore couch could not be the original word. Again this doesn't make much difference in English, but how does it change the underlying meaning in the original text.

Luke 5:19

19 And when they could not find by what way they might bring him in because of the multitude, they went upon the housetop, and let him down through the tiling with his couch into the midst before Jesus.

Luke 5:24

24 But that ye may know that the Son of man hath power upon earth to forgive sins, (he said unto the sick of the palsy,) I say unto thee, Arise, and take up thy couch, and go into thine house.

There are two more passages where the word couch has been inserted, but in both instances it is referring to the bodily position or posture as in couching down, no apparently change in meaning in the English.

Genesis 49:9

The Great Deception of the Mandela Effect

9 Judah is a lion's whelp: from the prey, my son, thou art went up: he stooped down, he couched as a lion, and as an old lion; who shall rouse him up?

Genesis 49:14
Issachar is a strong ass couching down between two burdens:

In the next passage, Exodus 13:12 the word matrix replaces the word womb. Not only does it make the passage sound unnatural, it minimizes the importance of the animals referred to in the passage, makes them into something less than a living creature.

Exodus 13:12 "That thou shalt set apart unto the Lord all that openeth the matrix, and every firstling that cometh of a beast which thou hast; the males shall be the Lord's."

The same change is made in Exodus 13:15 referring to the firstborn humans as well as animals with the same effect minimizing the importance and the humanity of the firstborn male children.

The Great Deception of the Mandela Effect

Exodus 13:15 "And it came to pass, when Pharaoh would hardly let us go, that the Lord slew all the firstborn in the land of Egypt, both the firstborn of man, and the firstborn of beast: therefore I sacrifice to the Lord all that openeth the matrix, being males; but all the firstborn of my children I redeem."

Exodus 24:12 "And the Lord said unto Moses, Come up to me into the mount, and be there: and I will give thee tables of stone, and a law, and commandments which I have written; that thou mayest teach them. Here we have tablets being replaced with tables in the next few passages.

Exodus 32:16
16 And the tables were the work of God, and the writing was the writing of God, graven upon the tables.

The Great Deception of the Mandela Effect

Exodus 32:19

19 And it came to pass, as soon as he came nigh unto the camp, that he saw the calf, and the dancing: and Moses' anger waxed hot, and he cast the tables out of his hands, and brake them beneath the mount.

Exodus 34:1

34 And the Lord said unto Moses, Hew thee two tables of stone like unto the first: and I will write upon these tables the words that were in the first tables, which thou brakest.

Exodus 34:4

4 And he hewed two tables of stone like unto the first; and Moses rose up early in the morning, and went up unto mount Sinai, as the Lord had commanded him, and took in his hand the two tables of stone.

Exodus 34:28

The Great Deception of the Mandela Effect

28 And he was there with the Lord forty days and forty nights; he did neither eat bread nor drink water. And he wrote upon the tables the words of the covenant, the ten commandments.

Exodus 34:29
29 And it came to pass, when Moses came down from mount Sinai with the two tables of testimony in Moses' hand, when he came down from the mount, that Moses wist not that the skin of his face shone while he talked with him.

Job 19:23: "Oh that my words were now written! Oh that they were printed in a book!" Used to read: Oh that my words were now written! Oh that they were written in a scroll!"

The word stuff has been added to the text in several places replacing belongings, it just sounds odd. Again I suspect the changes in the original language carries more weight.

Ezekial 12:3

The Great Deception of the Mandela Effect

3 Therefore, thou son of man, prepare thee stuff for removing, and remove by day in their sight; and thou shalt remove from thy place to another place in their sight: it may be they will consider, though they be a rebellious house.

Ezekiel 12:4

4 Then shalt thou bring forth thy stuff by day in their sight, as stuff for removing: and thou shalt go forth at even in their sight, as they that go forth into captivity.

Ezekiel 12:7

7 And I did so as I was commanded: I brought forth my stuff by day, as stuff for captivity, and in the even, I dug through the wall with mine hand; I brought it forth in the twilight, and I bare it upon my shoulder in their sight.

Tires did not exist in the time of Ezekiel, in fact, they were not invented until Robert William Thomson (1822 - 1873) invented the actual first vulcanized rubber pneumatic tire. Thomson patented his pneumatic tire in 1845.

The Great Deception of the Mandela Effect

Ezekiel 24:23 And your tires shall be upon your heads, and your shoes upon your feet: ye shall not mourn nor weep, but ye shall pine away for your iniquities, and mourn one toward another.

The addition of tires to this verse seems to me to display an evil sense of humor as Mandella would have his political enemies necklaced as an example to his followers. Necklacing someone entailed putting a rubber tire filled with gasoline over someone's head then setting it on fire, thereby burning the poor soul to death.

Isaiah 3:18

18 In that day the Lord will take away the bravery of their tinkling ornaments about their feet, and their cauls, and their round tires like the moon,

Isaiah 3:19

19 The chains, and the bracelets, and the mufflers,

Isaiah 7:3

The Great Deception of the Mandela Effect

3 Then said the Lord unto Isaiah, Go forth now to meet Ahaz, thou, and Shearjashub thy son, at the end of the conduit of the upper pool in the highway of the fuller's field;

Isaiah 13:21

21 But wild beasts of the desert shall lie there, and their houses shall be full of doleful creatures, and owls shall dwell there, and satyrs shall dance there.

Isaiah 11:8

8 And the sucking child shall play on the hole of the asp, and the weaned child shall put his hand on the cockatrice' den. (A cockatrice is a mythical beast, essentially a two-legged dragon or serpent-like creature with a cock's head) Wikipedia

Isaiah 11:16

16 And there shall be a highway for the remnant of his people, which shall be left, from Assyria; like as it was to Israel in the day that he came up out of the land of Egypt.

The Great Deception of the Mandela Effect

Isaiah 19:23

23 In that day shall there be a highway out of Egypt to Assyria, and the Assyrian shall come into Egypt, and the Egyptian into Assyria, and the Egyptians shall serve with the Assyrians.

Isaiah 33:8

8 The highways lie waste, the wayfaring man ceaseth: he hath broken the covenant, he hath despised the cities, he regardeth no man.

Isaiah 34:14

14 The wild beasts of the desert shall also meet with the wild beasts of the island, and the satyr shall cry to his fellow; the screech owl also shall rest there, and find for herself a place of rest.

Isaiah 35:8

8 And a highway shall be there, and a way, and it shall be called The way of holiness; the unclean shall not pass over

The Great Deception of the Mandela Effect

it; but it shall be for those: the wayfaring men, though fools, shall not err therein.

Isaiah 36:2

2 And the king of Assyria sent Rabshakeh from Lachish to Jerusalem unto king Hezekiah with a great army. And he stood by the conduit of the upper pool in the highway of the fuller's field.

Isaiah 40:3

3 The voice of him that crieth in the wilderness, Prepare ye the way of the Lord, make straight in the desert a highway for our God.

Isaiah 44:13

13 The carpenter stretcheth out his rule; he marketh it out with a line; he fitteth it with planes, and he marketh it out with the compass, and maketh it after the figure of a man, according to the beauty of a man; that it may remain in the house.

The Great Deception of the Mandela Effect

Isaiah 49:11

11 And I will make all my mountains a way, and my highways shall be exalted.

Isaiah 61:5

And strangers shall stand and feed your flocks, and the sons of the alien shall be your plowmen and your vinedressers.

Isaiah 62:10

10 Go through, go through the gates; prepare ye the way of the people; cast up, cast up the highway; gather out the stones; lift up a standard for the people.

Isaiah 65:25

25 The wolf and the lamb shall feed together, and the lion shall eat straw like the bullock: and dust shall be the serpent's meat. They shall not hurt nor destroy in all my holy mountain, saith the Lord.

Ecclesiastes 10:19 A feast is made for laughter, and wine maketh merry: **but money answereth all things.** Somehow

The Great Deception of the Mandela Effect

this passage claiming money answers all things seems out of step with the bible I know and love, but the passage does reinforce the money loving message of many of the apostate mega churches prominent these days. Again the mandella effect appears to be attacking traditional Christianity and promoting secularism.

17 Neither do men put new wine into old bottles: else the bottles break, and the wine runneth out, and the bottles perish: but they put new wine into new bottles, and both are preserved.

Matthew 22:9
9 Go ye therefore into the highways, and as many as ye shall find, bid to the marriage.

Matthew 22:10
10 So those servants went out into the highways, and gathered together all as many as they found, both bad and good: and the wedding was furnished with guests.

The Great Deception of the Mandela Effect

Mark 2:22 And no man putteth new wine into old bottles: else the new wine doth burst the bottles, and the wine is spilled, and the bottles will be marred: but new wine must be put into new bottles.

Mark 10:46
46 And they came to Jericho: and as he went out of Jericho with his disciples and a great number of people, blind Bartimaeus, the son of Timaeus, sat by the highway side begging.

Mark 13:10...." the gospel must first be preached in among all nations" Preached is now "published".
10 And the gospel must first be published among all nations.

Luke 1:35
35And the angel answered and said unto her, The Holy Ghost shall come upon thee, and the power of the Highest

shall overshadow thee: therefore also that holy thing which shall be born of thee shall be called the Son of God.

Luke 6:49

49But he that heareth, and doeth not, is like a man that without a foundation built a house upon the earth; against which the stream did beat vehemently, and immediately it fell, and the ruin of that house was great. This passage originally referred to building a house on sand, not on earth.

Luke 12:24

24 Consider the ravens: for they neither sow nor reap; which neither have storehouse nor barn; and God feedeth them: how much more are ye better than the fowls?

Luke 12:51

51 Suppose ye that I am come to give peace on earth? I tell you, Nay; but rather division:

Luke 14:10

The Great Deception of the Mandela Effect

But when thou art bidden, go and sit down in the lowest room; that when he that bade thee cometh, he may say unto thee, Friend, go up higher: then shalt thou have worship in the presence of them that sit at meat with thee.

Luke 14:23

23And the lord said unto the servant, Go out into the highways and hedges, and compel them to come in, that my house may be filled.

Luke 17:31

31 In that day, he which shall be upon the housetop, and his stuff in the house, let him not come down to take it away: and he that is in the field, let him likewise not return back.

Luke 18:30

30Who shall not receive manifold more in this present time, and in the world to come life everlasting.

Luke 19:23

The Great Deception of the Mandela Effect

23 Wherefore then gavest not thou my money into the bank, that at my coming I might have required mine own with usury?

Luke 19:27 "Show" has been replaced with "SLAY" them before me"
27 But those mine enemies, which would not that I should reign over them, bring hither, and slay them before me.

Acts 5:15
Insomuch that they brought forth the sick into the streets, and laid them on beds and couches, that at the least the shadow of Peter passing by might overshadow some of them.

Ephesians 2:12 12 That at that time ye were without Christ, being aliens from the commonwealth of Israel, and strangers from the covenants of promise, having no hope, and without God in the world: (strangers was replaced with aliens)

Hebrews 9:26

The Great Deception of the Mandela Effect

26 For then must he often have suffered since the foundation of the world: but now once in the end of the world hath he appeared to put away sin by the sacrifice of himself.

Hebrews 11:34
34 Quenched the violence of fire, escaped the edge of the sword, out of weakness were made strong, waxed valiant in fight, turned to flight the armies of the aliens.

Revelations 22:12…Reads "according as his work shall be" and I remember according to his work.

Job 19:23 changes scroll or tablet to book, books, of course, are something that would not be developed until after the Christian church came into existence. "Oh that my words were now written! oh that they were printed in a book!" In this instance, the mandella change doesn't appear to be of any importance only an oddity that still carries the meaning of the original text.

The Great Deception of the Mandela Effect

psalm 119:2 Blessed are they that keep his testimonies, and that seek him with the whole heart. This verse changes Commandments to testimonies. Testimonies obviously do not carry the same weight as commandments. Testimonies can be taken left as one chooses. Commandments on the other hand had better be adhered to.

Isaiah 11:6 is the verse that first brought my attention to mandella effect changes in the bible. Isaiah 11:6 currently reads "The wolf also shall dwell with the lamb, and the leopard shall lie down with the kid; and the calf and the young lion and the fatling together, and a little child shall lead them." My memory of this beloved verse is The lion shall lay down with the lamb... This change is blatant and most definitely alters the meaning of the original text, both metaphorically and literally. Not only is a lion a large predator and a lamb easy prey, but the lion is a symbol of Christ as in the Lion of Judah, and the lamb is also a symbol of Christ as in the Lamb of God who takes away the sins of the world. The Lion of Judah and the Lamb of God are one and the same in Jesus Christ! Now the passage just reads

The Great Deception of the Mandela Effect

"The wolf also shall dwell with the lamb," which means nothing more than the predator wolf lives near its source of food, the lamb. The passage now is no different than saying the fox is in the hen house!

Isaiah 65:25 The wolf and the lamb shall feed together, and the lion shall eat straw like the bullock: and dust shall be the serpent's meat. They shall not hurt nor destroy in all my holy mountain, saith the Lord. This passage also as I recall was the lion and the lamb, but at least it appears to maintain the original meaning.

Matthew 7:1 Judge not, that ye be not judged.

Matthew 6:9-13 After this manner, therefore, pray ye: Our Father which art in heaven, Hallowed be thy name. Thy kingdom come. Thy will be done in earth, as it is in heaven. Give us this day our daily bread. And forgive us our debts, as we forgive our debtors. And lead us not into temptation, but deliver us from evil: For thine is the kingdom, and the power, and the glory, for ever. Amen. On earth instead of in earth and Trespasses rather than debts

Matthew 9:17 Neither do men put new wine into old bottles: else the bottles break, and the wine runneth out, and the bottles perish: but they put new wine into new bottles, and both are preserved. Wineskins

Matthew 21:6-8 And the disciples went, and did as Jesus commanded them, 7 And brought the ass, and the colt, and put on them their clothes, and they set him thereon. 8 And a very great multitude spread their garments in the way; others cut down branches from the trees, and strawed them in the way. Donkey or ass no colt

Mark 1:7 And preached, saying, There cometh one mightier than I after me, the latchet of whose shoes I am not worthy to stoop down and unloose. I am not worthy to stoop down and untie the thong of his sandals.

The Great Deception of the Mandela Effect

Mark 2:22 And no man putteth new wine into old bottles: else the new wine doth burst the bottles, and the wine is spilled, and the bottles will be marred: but new wine must be put into new bottles wineskins

Mark 13:10 And the gospel must first be published among all nations. Preached among all nations

Luke 1:35 And the angel answered and said unto her, The Holy Ghost shall come upon thee, and the power of the Highest shall overshadow thee: therefore also that holy thing which shall be born of thee shall be called the Son of God. Holy One, not holy thing

Luke 6:49 But he that heareth, and doeth not, is like a man that without a foundation built a house upon the earth; against which the stream did beat vehemently, and immediately it fell, and the ruin of that house was great. Sand, not earth

The Great Deception of the Mandela Effect

Luke 12:24 Consider the ravens: for they neither sow nor reap; which neither have storehouse nor barn; and God feedeth them: how much more are ye better than the fowls? (ravens instead of sparrows)

Luke 17:31 In that day, he which shall be upon the housetop, and his stuff in the house, let him not come down to take it away: and he that is in the field, let him likewise not return back.

Luke 19:23 Wherefore then gavest not thou my money into the bank, that at my coming I might have required mine own with usury?

Luke 19:27 But those mine enemies, which would not that I should reign over them, bring hither, and slay them before me.

John 8:32 And ye shall know the truth, and the truth shall make you free. Set you free, not make you free

The Great Deception of the Mandela Effect

Revelations 22:12 And, behold, I come quickly; and my reward is with me, to give every man according as his work shall be. (Render according to his work?)

Last, in this section I am listing examples of words currently in the KJV of the bible that I am sure were never there before. The verses are listed so you can look them up in your own bibles. I recommend comparing different versions of the bible because at this point in time not all versions contain the same errors.

As I recall unicorns are mythical creatures that were never mentioned in the bible. Some verse listed here replace oxen with unicorns.

Numbers 23:22 God brought them out of Egypt; he hath as it were the strength of a unicorn.

Numbers 24:8 God brought him forth out of Egypt; he hath as it were the strength of a unicorn: he shall eat up the

The Great Deception of the Mandela Effect

nations his enemies, and shall break their bones, and pierce them through with his arrows.

Deuteronomy 33:17 His glory is like the firstling of his bullock, and his horns are like the horns of unicorns: with them, he shall push the people together to the ends of the earth: and they are the ten thousands of Ephraim, and they are the thousands of Manasseh.

Job 39:9 Will the unicorn be willing to serve thee, or abide by thy crib?

Job 39:10 Canst thou bind the unicorn with his band in the furrow? or will he harrow the valleys after thee?

Psalms 22:21 Save me from the lion's mouth: for thou hast heard me from the horns of the unicorns.

Psalms 29:6 He maketh them also to skip like a calf; Lebanon and Sirion like a young unicorn.

The Great Deception of the Mandela Effect

Psalms 92:10 But my horn shalt thou exalt like the horn of a unicorn: I shall be anointed with fresh oil.

Isaiah 34:7 And the unicorns shall come down with them, and the bullocks with the bulls; and their land shall be soaked with blood, and their dust made fat with fatness.

bottles Wineskins and jars have been replaced with bottles!

Joshua 9:4 They did work wilily, and went and made as if they had been ambassadors, and took old sacks upon their asses, and wine-bottles, old, and rent, and bound up;

Joshua 9:13 And these bottles of wine, which we filled, were new; and, behold, they be rent: and these our garments and our shoes are become old by reason of the very long journey.

I Samuel 25:18 Then Abigail made haste, and took two hundred loaves, and two bottles of wine, and five sheep ready dressed, and five measures of parched corn, and an

The Great Deception of the Mandela Effect

hundred clusters of raisins, and two hundred cakes of figs, and laid them on asses.

Job 32:19 Behold, my belly is as wine which hath no vent; it is ready to burst like new bottles.

Job 38:37 Who can number the clouds in wisdom? or who can stay the bottles of heaven,

Jeremiah 48:12 Therefore, behold, the days come, saith the Lord, that I will send unto him wanderers, that shall cause him to wander, and shall empty his vessels, and break their bottles.

Hosea 7:5 In the day of our king the princes have made him sick with bottles of wine; he stretched out his hand with scorners.

Matthew 9:17 Neither do men put new wine into old bottles: else the bottles break, and the wine runneth out, and the

The Great Deception of the Mandela Effect

bottles perish: but they put new wine into new bottles, and both are preserved.

Mark 2:22 And no man putteth new wine into old bottles: else the new wine doth burst the bottles, and the wine is spilled, and the bottles will be marred: but new wine must be put into new bottles.

Luke 5:37 And no man putteth new wine into old bottles; else the new wine will burst the bottles, and be spilled, and the bottles shall perish.

Luke 5:38 But new wine must be put into new bottles, and both are preserved.

slay

Luke 19:27 But those mine enemies, which would not that I should reign over them, bring hither, and slay them before me.

The Great Deception of the Mandela Effect

Easter was a pagan holiday, not celebrated by the Jews, nor Christ, nor the apostles – they celebrated Passover, yet in Acts 12:4 the King James bible now reads
"And when he had apprehended him, he put him in prison, and delivered him to four quaternions of soldiers to keep him; intending after Easter to bring him forth to the people."

matrix word womb is replaced with the word matrix! Whoever or whatever is doing this must be laughing over this one!

Isaiah 13:21King James Version (KJV)
21 But wild beasts of the desert shall lie there, and their houses shall be full of doleful creatures; and owls shall dwell there, and satyrs shall dance there.

Isaiah 34:14King James Version (KJV)
14 The wild beasts of the desert shall also meet with the wild beasts of the island, and the satyr shall cry to his fellow; the screech owl also shall rest there, and find for herself a place of rest.

The Great Deception of the Mandela Effect

The word foreigner has been changed to alien in the following passages.

Deuteronomy 14:21
Ye shall not eat of anything that dieth of itself: thou shalt give it unto the stranger that is within thy gates, that he may eat it; or thou mayest sell it unto an alien: for thou art a holy people unto the Lord thy God. Thou shalt not seethe a kid in his mother's milk.

Job 19:15
They that dwell in mine house, and my maids, count me for a stranger: I am an alien in their sight.

Psalm 69:8
I become a stranger unto my brethren, and an alien unto my mother's children.

Lamentations 5:2
Our inheritance is turned to strangers, our houses to aliens.

The Great Deception of the Mandela Effect

Ephesians 2:12

That at that time ye were without Christ, being aliens from the commonwealth of Israel, and strangers from the covenants of promise, having no hope, and without God in the world:

Hebrews 11:34

Quenched the violence of fire, escaped the edge of the sword, out of weakness were made strong, waxed valiant in fight, turned to flight the armies of the aliens.

Again the word womb has been replaced with the word matrix in the next passages.

Exodus 13:12

That thou shalt set apart unto the Lord all that openeth the matrix, and every firstling that cometh of a beast which thou hast; the males shall be the Lord's.

Exodus 13:15

The Great Deception of the Mandela Effect

And it came to pass, when Pharaoh would hardly let us go, that the Lord slew all the firstborn in the land of Egypt, both the firstborn of man, and the firstborn of beast: therefore I sacrifice to the Lord all that openeth the matrix, being males; but all the firstborn of my children I redeem.

Exodus 34:19
All that openeth the matrix is mine; and every firstling among thy cattle, whether ox or sheep, that is male.

Numbers 3:12
And I, behold, I have taken the Levites from among the children of Israel instead of all the firstborn that openeth the matrix among the children of Israel: therefore the Levites shall be mine;

Numbers 18:15
Every thing that openeth the matrix in all flesh, which they bring unto the Lord, whether it be of men or beasts, shall be thine: nevertheless the firstborn of man shalt thou surely

The Great Deception of the Mandela Effect

redeem, and the firstling of unclean beasts shalt thou redeem.

In Context | Full Chapter | Other Translation

The Word "Stuff" has now replaced possessions and belongs.

Genesis 31:37

Whereas thou hast searched all my stuff, what hast thou found of all thy household stuff? set it here before my brethren and thy brethren, that they may judge betwixt us both.

Genesis 45:20

Also, regard not your stuff; for the good of all the land of Egypt is yours.

Exodus 22:7

If a man shall deliver unto his neighbor money or stuff to keep, and it be stolen out of the man's house; if the thief is found, let him pay double.

The Great Deception of the Mandela Effect

Exodus 36:7

For the stuff they had was sufficient for all the work to make it, and too much.

Joshua 7:11

Israel hath sinned, and they have also transgressed my covenant which I commanded them: for they have even taken of the accursed thing, and have also stolen, and dissembled also, and they have put it even among their own stuff.

1 Samuel 10:22

Therefore they enquired of the Lord further, if the man should yet come thither. And the Lord answered, Behold he hath hid himself among the stuff.

1 Samuel 25:13

And David said unto his men, Gird ye on every man his sword. And they girded on every man his sword, and David also girded on his sword: and there went up after David about four hundred men; and two hundred abodes by the stuff.

1 Samuel 30:24
For who will hearken unto you in this matter? but as his part is that goeth down to the battle, so shall his part be that tarrieth by the stuff: they shall part alike.

Nehemiah 13:8
And it grieved me sore: therefore I cast forth all the household stuff to Tobiah out of the chamber.

Ezekiel 12:3
Therefore, thou son of man, prepare thee stuff for removing, and remove by day in their sight; and thou shalt remove from thy place to another place in their sight: it may be they will consider, though they be a rebellious house.

Ezekiel 12:4

The Great Deception of the Mandela Effect

Then shalt thou bring forth thy stuff by day in their sight, as stuff for removing: and thou shalt go forth at even in their sight, as they that go forth into captivity.

Ezekiel 12:7

And I did so as I was commanded: I brought forth my stuff by day, as stuff for captivity, and in the even, I dug through the wall with mine hand; I brought it forth in the twilight, and I bare it upon my shoulder in their sight.

Luke 17:31

In that day, he which shall be upon the housetop, and his stuff in the house, let him not come down to take it away: and he that is in the field, let him likewise not return back.

The nonsensical phrase "nursing father" has been added to the book of Numbers.

Numbers 11:12 Have I conceived all these people? have I begotten them, that thou shouldest say unto me, Carry them in thy bosom, as a nursing father beareth the sucking child, unto the land which thou squarest unto their fathers?

The word "Unicorn" has replaced "wild ox or oxen in the following passages.

Numbers 23:22
God brought them out of Egypt; he hath as it were the strength of a unicorn.

Numbers 24:8
God brought him forth out of Egypt; he hath as it were the strength of a unicorn: he shall eat up the nations his enemies, and shall break their bones, and pierce them through with his arrows.

Deuteronomy 33:17
His glory is like the firstling of his bullock, and his horns are like the horns of unicorns: with them, he shall push the people together to the ends of the earth: and they are the ten

The Great Deception of the Mandela Effect

thousands of Ephraim, and they are the thousands of Manasseh.

Job 39:9

Will the unicorn be willing to serve thee, or abide by thy crib?

Job 39:10

Canst thou bind the unicorn with his band in the furrow? or will he harrow the valleys after thee?

Psalm 22:21

Save me from the lion's mouth: for thou hast heard me from the horns of the unicorns.

Psalm 29:6

He maketh them also to skip like a calf; Lebanon and Sirion like a young unicorn.

The Great Deception of the Mandela Effect

Psalm 92:10

But my horn shalt thou exalts like the horn of a unicorn: I shall be anointed with fresh oil.

Isaiah 34:7

And the unicorns shall come down with them, and the bullocks with the bulls; and their land shall be soaked with blood, and their dust made fat with fatness.

A cockatrice is a mythical creature, essentially a two-legged dragon with a rooster's head. The cockatrice was first described in the late fourteenth century. However, the Mandella Effect has added this mythical creature "Cockatrice" has been included in the following passages.

Isaiah 11:8

And the sucking child shall play on the hole of the asp, and the weaned child shall put his hand on the cockatrice' den.

Isaiah 14:29

The Great Deception of the Mandela Effect

Rejoice not thou, whole Palestina, because the rod of him that smote thee is broken: for out of the serpent's root shall come forth a cockatrice, and his fruit shall be a fiery flying serpent.

Isaiah 59:5
They hatch cockatrice' eggs, and weave the spider's web: he that eateth of their eggs dieth, and that which is crushed breaketh out into a viper.

Jeremiah 8:17
For, behold, I will send serpents, cockatrices, among you, which will not be charmed, and they shall bite you, saith the Lord.

Speaking of mythical beasts satyrs are now included in the following passages. I personally believe that these mythical beasts being added to scripture are intended to discount and devalue the bible.

Isaiah 13:21

The Great Deception of the Mandela Effect

But wild beasts of the desert shall lie there, and their houses shall be full of doleful creatures; and owls shall dwell there, and satyrs shall dance there.

Isaiah 34:14
The wild beasts of the desert shall also meet with the wild beasts of the island, and the satyr shall cry to his fellow; the screech owl also shall rest there, and find for herself a place of rest.

So far we have talked about mandella effect changes within the King James Bible. Changes of one word for another, one phrase for another, even the addition of mythical creatures, but are those the only changes? And is the King James Bible the only version of scripture affected? Don't bet on it. Below is a list of bible passages that remain in the King James bible, but have disappeared from other versions of the bible, not all, but some. I looked these passages up in several different translations and found them included in some, but gone in others. What I found most odd is that in the Bibles that do not retains these verses the verses

The Great Deception of the Mandela Effect

have vanished. That is not only are they not included in that version, but the verse number is gone too. For an example in my copy of the New International version of the bible Matthew 17:20 skips Matthew 17:21 and goes straight to Matthew 17:22! I found it to follow the same pattern in all of the verses in all of the versions where the verses are missing. These verses were included in my King James version, Amplified, and New American Study Bible, but missing in others. I suggest you take a look for yourself.

I know that the mandella effect changes are not limited to those I have listed. I realize that new Mandela effect changes are discovered almost daily by people all over the world. I also know that all too often changes discovered are sometimes nothing more than mistaken memories. I believe that some of you will agree that many of these changes have occurred while at the same time not accept that others have taken place. I am certain that some scripture passages do not agree with what you remember from the bible and perhaps some of them do. Just as some people remember the Scarecrow from the wizard of Oz brandishing

The Great Deception of the Mandela Effect

a revolver while others do not. Finally, I am painfully aware that with every changed discovered and noted with residual evidence or not the material evidence will support that what is always was the way it is no matter what our individual experience. I watched a youtube video the other day posted by meegs b, that discussed changes she found in the book of Job, specifically Job 6:6. where it is discussing the tastelessness of eggwhite. I certainly agree with meegs that I never read any mention of egg whites in the book of Job, or anywhere in scripture for that matter. To further confuse the issue when looking at other translations of the bible one can discover what may have been the original meaning of the verse, but also even more bizarre meanings. Such as in the Lexham English Bible, where it reads "Can tasteless food be eaten without[a] salt, or is there taste in the white of a marshmallow plant?" I for one have never heard of such a thing as a marshmallow plant. I share this bit with my son, who tends to be skeptical of all things Mandela, did a quick search and showed me that yes there is, in fact, such a thing as a marshmallow plant, always has been! So it goes with the Mandela effect. If one is seeking physical proof that it exists

The Great Deception of the Mandela Effect

and is not merely an immense example of confabulation, I fear one is destined to failure.

I can't explain the differences in perception and memory involved. I do not know if experiments at CERN are responsible, or if some secret government experiments in time travel are affecting history. I can't even claim to know if this is a matter of mass hypnosis or some other form of mind control. There are many theories attempting to explain this issue. Personally, I tend to look for the spiritual underlying the material experience and in this instance do suspect deception lays at the root of it all. Satanic Deception designed to lead the elect astray if at all possible in this critical point in time.

The Great Deception of the Mandela Effect

The Great Deception of the Mandela Effect

Chapter Five

After taking a look at many of the possible changes some of us are aware of, changes both in the secular world and in the bible it may be time for us to reconsider how committed we are to our view of reality. What is reality after all? It is all to easy to simply say it is the sum total of all that is real, but in truth that doesn't tell us a thing. That is like those who are not aware of the changes simply "saying you are misremembering it it", or "it has always been this way" If one considers atomic structure one will understand that no matter how real physical reality appears it is mostly empty space, nothing more than a number of electrons orbiting their neutron with vast space in between, but that is not what we perceive, is it? If we consider quantum mechanics it gets a little bit deeper, a little bit stranger.

Doctor Jeff Zweerink suggests that quantum mechanics "offers a more radical solution based on the existence of a

The Great Deception of the Mandela Effect

multiverse. These models propose that a repulsive force exists between particles in each of the clones in parallel universes. This repulsive force causes ripples to propagate through all the parallel universes, leading to the weird effects seen in quantum experiments. Computer simulations with 41 such universes reproduce many of these "quantum" effects, including those of the iconic double-slit experiment, and the level of agreement increases with the number of parallel worlds. This suggests the intriguing possibility that future research may determine the number of parallel worlds in the multiverse.1

At this point, no one knows the final answer to the question, what is the ultimate nature of reality? Maybe things really exist simultaneously in different states or maybe not. Perhaps quantum effects simply result from interacting multiverses."

After all how can it be possible for things we know and remember to have changed and not just change in recent history but to have changed from the beginning? What is the reality that such a thing can occur? Does this begin to explain what people experience that we call the Mandella

The Great Deception of the Mandela Effect

Effect? Or is it a matter of some deep governmental agency experimenting with mind control practicing the new art of removing old memories and implanting new ones more to the liking of the ruling class whoever they may be.

What is the root cause behind the Mandela Effect changes to reality? And what is the reason behind that cause? Is there a Luciferian cult actively trying to tear the veil between realities and release the fallen angels including Satan himself. Some suggest that the activities at CERN are designed to cause just this phenomenon. Many believe that their experiments have already as a byproduct caused all manner of negative events. Whether CERN has been able to open a portal is unknown, but this has been suggested as a possible cause of the Mandela effect. Personally I believe all things no matter what have a spiritual underpinning. The scientists at CERN may or may not be trying to open a portal to hell, but whatever their goal. if they are part of the Mandela Effect it is due to an ancient conflict of a supernatural nature.

Before we go further, let us take a moment to consider how we perceive the world around us. Let us consider our

The Great Deception of the Mandela Effect

five senses. Scientists have given each of our senses a very specific name taken from Latin and ancient Greek, in part to precisely describe our senses, but also to include them in their own particular vocabulary of jargon. Some senses so named include ophthalmoception, or the sense of sight, audioception, or the sense of sound, gustaoception, or the sense of taste, olfacoception, or the sense of smell, and tactioception, or the sense of touch. These are what are commonly called our five senses. There are other senses we rely on such as thermoception, or the sense of temperature, proprioceptionor, the sense of motion, equilibrioception, the sense of balance, and nociception, the sense of pain. It is through our senses that we experience the world we live in, but our senses have limits and we are not able to perceive all that is there is in the world to perceive.

   Studies have indicated that cattle and deer are aware of and aline themselves and feed along the Earth's magnetic fields and that bees can sense the negative electrical fields surrounding flowers. Dogs have a much stronger sense of smell than we do, as well as a far more acute sense of hearing. Cats have a much better sense of sight and can see

The Great Deception of the Mandela Effect

clearly in the dark what we cannot see. Anyone who has ever had a pet cat or dog will tell you that on occasion they appear to be aware of things we simply cannot see or hear.

In the book of Numbers, there is recorded the story of Balaam and his ass. Numbers 22:23 "And the ass saw the angel of Jehovah standing in the way, with his sword drawn in his hand; and the ass turned aside out-of-the-way, and went into the field: and Balaam smote the ass, to turn her into the way. Then the angel of Jehovah stood in a narrow path between the vineyards, a wall being on this side, and a wall on that side. And the ass saw the angel of Jehovah, and she thrust herself unto the wall and crushed Balaam's foot against the wall: and he smote her again. And the angel of Jehovah went further and stood in a narrow place, where was no way to turn either to the right hand or to the left. And the ass saw the angel of Jehovah, and she lay down under Balaam: and Balaam's anger was kindled, and he smote the ass with his staff. And Jehovah opened the mouth of the ass, and she said unto Balaam, What have I done unto thee, that thou hast smitten me these three times? And Balaam said unto the ass,   Because thou hast mocked me, I would there

The Great Deception of the Mandela Effect

be a sword in my hand, for now, I had killed thee. And the ass said unto Balaam, Am not I thine ass, upon which thou hast rode all thy life long unto this day? Was I ever wont to do so unto thee? And he said, Nay. Then Jehovah opened the eyes of Balaam, and he saw the angel of Jehovah standing in the way, with his sword drawn in his hand; and he bowed his head, and fell on his face. And the angel of Jehovah said unto him, Wherefore hast thou smitten thine ass these three times? Behold, I am come forth for an adversary because thy way is perverse before me: and the ass saw me, and turned aside before me these three times: unless she had turned aside from me, surely now I had even slain thee, and saved her alive." As you can see from the story the ass clearly saw the angel of Jehovah blocking his master's way. There is a miracle recorded here, but it is not that the ass saw the angel, it is that Jehovah opened the mouth of the ass and let him speak and perhaps there is a second miracle in that Jehovah opened Balaam's eyes allowing him to see the angel of Jehovah.

Speaking of our senses, there is also what some call the sixth sense or extrasensory perception. Many people practice

The Great Deception of the Mandela Effect

hours of meditation attempting to heighten their psychic abilities so that they may become aware of those things not normally visible to the human eye nor audible to the human ear. Extrasensory perception comes in and out of vogue with each new generation always being promoted as something new and different, but the truth be told, channelers are no different from yesterday's mediums, and the new age is as old as the mystery religions of ancient Babylon. Be that as it may be, many people study occult literature and practice meditation in the hopes of developing their senses to the point that they may delve into unseen realities.

So what is the point I am so painstakingly trying to make? It is best summed up by William Shakespeare in Hamlet where Hamlet says to Horatio "There are more things in heaven and earth, Horatio, Than are dreamt of in your philosophy."

According to quantum mechanics, there must be at least ten dimensions, possibly as many as twenty-six. The well known Bible scholar Chuck Missler states in "The Boundaries of Reality"

The Great Deception of the Mandela Effect

that "The ancient Hebrew scholar Nachmonides, writing in the 12th century, concluded from his studies of the text of Genesis that the universe has ten dimensions: that four are knowable and six are beyond our knowing. "

He continues further stating that "Particle physicists today have also concluded that we live in ten dimensions. Three spatial dimensions and time are directly discernible and measurable. The remaining six are "curled" in less than the Planck length (10-33 centimeters) and thus are only inferable by indirect means."

(Some physicists believe that there may be as many as 26 dimensions. Ten and twenty-six emerge from the mathematics associated with superstring theory, a current candidate in the pursuit of a theory to totally integrate all known forces in the universe.) "

    These dimensions consist of the three we are normally aware of plus time as the fourth and then six others. This works out mathematically and answers some theoretical questions Albert Einstein did not have time to resolve before he passed away. You can find descriptions of the remaining six dimensions with a little bit of research. I don't claim to be

The Great Deception of the Mandela Effect

a physicist, in fact, I confess to being woefully ignorant in such matters beyond a popular understanding, but I can see that these recent discoveries confirm my belief that we are woefully limited in our perception of the universe. I personally suspect that the book of Genesis is more accurate than it is normally given credit for in our generation. As a matter of speculation on my part, I suspect that Adam and Eve did, in fact, die spiritually when they ate from the tree of the knowledge of good and evil and with that death lost all awareness of all dimensions except four. I imagine that they were literally clothed in light and were aware of that up until their spiritual death. At that time they were no longer able to see the spiritual and were shocked at seeing themselves as purely physical naked animal creatures. From that time onward we have been denied the perception of the spiritual dimensions of creation. It is not that we live in a world limited to three dimensions and time, that is not the case at all. We live in a world composed of however many dimensions there are, but we wander around blind and deaf to much of reality.

The Great Deception of the Mandela Effect

Simply put there are within creation dimensions our limited senses deny us the ability to perceive. We are not only unaware of those dimensions but are also unaware of the creatures that call such dimensions home. There are spiritual creatures that reside in these dimensions and are very well able of traveling within the four dimension we are able to perceive. These creatures may remain primarily invisible to us, or they may choose to show themselves in one form or another.

Why do I qualify invisible? I qualify the word invisible in this context because there are instances recorded in the Bible where angels appear to men not as spirits, but as physical entities. So although I am quite certain, that we are normally totally unaware of a spirit or an angel's presence beyond a vague feeling, or perhaps a fleeting glimpse, we are actually surrounded by spiritual beings much of the time. These spiritual beings may be attempting to do us either good, ill, or are ignoring us according to their will or the will of the One who sent them. They may simply be indulging their curiosity of how God's plan may be worked out in a particular circumstance.

The Great Deception of the Mandela Effect

Chapter Six

There is a celestial war going on all around us, surrounding us with spiritual violence and mayhem. It began with rebellion in the ranks of heaven and with the creation of man the fighting has moved to the Earth. So in effect, we have all been born in the midst of a supernatural war. Fierce battles raging everywhere we walk, with no place for us to hide from the carnage. When I was a boy this battle was often depicted in cartoons as a little devil sitting on one shoulder and a little angel sitting on the other shoulder of one of the cartoon characters. The little devil tempting the character to do something bad, and the little angel encouraging the character to do something good instead. As far as that goes it is correct, much of spiritual warfare involves our efforts to resist temptation, but that certainly is not all that there is to it.

It would be easy to scoff at the thought of a spiritual war going on all around us as we go through the day to day routine of our lives, but is it really all that hard to see? The

The Great Deception of the Mandela Effect

world is in chaos; riots in the streets, Muslims killing Christians around the world for the simple reason they are Christian. Muslim militias burning down churches and entire villages in Africa and the Middle East, kidnapping school girls to sell in the slave trade, Christians being imprisoned for the life of three generations for the crime of being Christian in North Korea. Clarification may be needed by what is meant by three generations; in North Korea, when one is convicted of being a Christian not only is that person sent to prison for life but that persons entire family will be imprisoned, grandparents, parents, and children for the duration of their lives. The communists are serious about stamping out those pesky Christians in North Korea. The church is routinely persecuted in communist countries, yet it survives even grows under such persecution.

One might say, that is all occurring in the middle east and in communist countries, but nothing like that is happening in the enlightened west. One could say that, but one would be wrong. The difference in the enlightened west and the rest of the world is only a matter of degree. People have been fired for wearing a cross on a chain around their neck while at

The Great Deception of the Mandela Effect

work. Christians are commonly the butt of jokes in the media. The right to practice one's religion, if that religion is Christianity, is under assault in the United States where the federal government is attempting to force Christian employers to provide abortion coverage for their employees and pastors risk losing the tax exempt status for their church if they should be so brazen as to take a politically incorrect stance from the pulpit. This morning I read an article about a five-year-old girl being reprimanded by a school official for saying grace before lunch at her school.

In the United States Christians aren't being beheaded or sentenced to prison for life, but they are not being tolerated as they once were. The United States today is a country where a girl can be expelled from a public school for saying bless you to a friend who has sneezed. The United States has fallen a long way from the vision of the founding fathers. The number of abortions performed each day is truly staggering bringing the total number of abortions since 1973 to 57,109,310 at the time of my writing this and there have been 703,547 so far this year. Worldwide the numbers total 1,345,813,501 innocents killed and counting.

The Great Deception of the Mandela Effect

Those are a few visible examples of the material effects of the unseen spiritual conflict going on behind the scenes in the world in which we live. You must understand that the spiritual comes before the material, just as a thought comes before an action, and although these conflicts appear as political, social, or military the underlying root cause of what we see as the culture war is spiritual in nature.
As Saint Paul clearly states in Ephesians 6:12 "For our wrestling is not against flesh and blood, but against the principalities, against the powers, against the world-rulers of this darkness, against the spiritual hosts of wickedness in the heavenly places." Our battle is not against the human rulers of this world. The politicians currently available to us may be so corrupt that the thought of them makes one want to vomit when it is time to participate in an election, but we must remember as disgusting as politicians are they are only the physical puppets enacting the policies of those holding their strings. The thrones, powers and principalities, the fallen angels and demons pulling the strings of the puppet politicians, those invisible combatants are who we truly face in battle. It is they who are at war with the church.

The Great Deception of the Mandela Effect

Now that I have mentioned the Church, that is the total congregation of Christians in the world. I am not referring to any particular denomination as in my opinion they are all equally apostate. The organized church has become a big business and has lost the saving truth of the gospel along the way in their attempts to attract an audience and contributions to their coffers.

One may think they are safe within the confines of the local church, but nothing can be further from the truth. Demons visit the churches at least if not more often than Christians do. Many of them inhabit high ranking clergy. How better to lead Christians away from the truth than to control the hierarchy of the church. Consider the European Bishop who is taking down the crosses from the churches so as to not offend Muslims. I have to wonder how often Muslims attend her churches, and if they do what good is it without Christ? That was only one example taken from the news, there are clown services where the clergy dress up as clowns, There is homosexual clergy promoting homosexuality and homosexual marriage within the church. There are the churches that worship financial prosperity

The Great Deception of the Mandela Effect

more than anything else, to name a few of the errors currently embraced by what I would have to call the secular church.

What is the secular church? You may ask. Quite simply it is the worldly church, it is the church that gave up Christ and redemption in favor of political correctness. These are the churches where everyone is welcome as it should b, but no one is held responsible, no one is reminded of their sins and the path to forgiveness and redemption through the cross. No one is encouraged to examine themselves and repent of their sins. They are in the case of homosexuality they are encouraged to glory in their sins. In the past decade or so the homosexual movement has engaged in an all-out assault against the church and in a large part has been victorious in driving orthodox Christians out or at the very least forcing them into silent submission. Again, you may be tempted to chalk this up to liberal politics, but in reality, this has its origin in the unseen spiritual realm. I personally rarely attend the secular church, but I do frequently worship at home, I'm told by friends and acquaintances that I am missing out on the fellowship at church and perhaps in a sense they are

The Great Deception of the Mandela Effect

right, but I look at fellowship of the church from a slightly different angle. I look at who Christ spent time with while on Earth. Even though he did go to the Temple, and to the synagogues I don't believe it was there that he found fellowship. I believe Christ found and offered fellowship to the outcasts of society, to the prostitutes and tax collectors. I believe he sought out the lost, but not the reprobate. I don't think he spent more time than he had to witness to the Pharisees and Sadducees. It seems to me that he spent no more time with the self-righteous of his day than he had to to to answer their charges against him and to bare witness to His Father.

Don't let me lead you into thinking that the secular church is the only place where one may be entertaining demons unaware, but before we delve into the traps laid for us by the evil one, let us stop and take a look at exactly who are enemies are. Before we discuss demons let us take a look at what are commonly called fallen angels.

2 Thessalonians 2:11-17 And for this cause God shall send them strong delusion, that they should believe a lie: That

The Great Deception of the Mandela Effect

they all might be damned who believed not the truth, but had pleasure in unrighteousness. But we are bound to give thanks alway to God for you, brethren beloved of the Lord because God hath from the beginning chosen you to salvation through sanctification of the Spirit and belief of the truth: Whereunto he called you by our gospel, to the obtaining of the glory of our Lord Jesus Christ. Therefore, brethren, stand fast and hold the traditions which ye have been taught, whether by word, or our epistle. Now our Lord Jesus Christ himself, and God, even our Father, which hath loved us, and hath given us everlasting consolation and good hope through grace, comfort your hearts, and establish you in every good word and work.

The revelation of John Chapter 12:7-17 And there was war in heaven: Michael and his angels fought against the dragon, and the dragon fought and his angels, And prevailed not; neither was their place found any more in heaven. And the great dragon was cast out, that old serpent, called the Devil, and Satan, which deceiveth the whole world: he was cast out into the earth, and his angels were cast out with him. And I

The Great Deception of the Mandela Effect

heard a loud voice saying in heaven, Now is come salvation, and strength, and the kingdom of our God, and the power of his Christ: for the accuser of our brethren is cast down, which accused them before our God day and night. And they overcame him by the blood of the Lamb, and by the word of their testimony, and they loved not their lives unto the death. Therefore rejoice, ye heavens, and ye that dwell in them. Woe to the inhabiters of the earth and of the sea! for the devil is come down unto you, having great wrath, because he knoweth that he hath but a short time. And when the dragon saw that he was cast unto the earth, he persecuted the woman which brought forth the manchild. And to the woman were given two wings of a great eagle, that she might fly into the wilderness, into her place, where she is nourished for a time, and times, and half a time, from the face of the serpent. And the serpent cast out of his mouth water as a flood after the woman, that he might cause her to be carried away of the flood. And the earth helped the woman, and the earth opened her mouth and swallowed up the flood which the dragon cast out of his mouth. And the dragon was wroth with the woman and went to make war with the remnant of her seed, which

The Great Deception of the Mandela Effect

keeps the commandments of God, and have the testimony of Jesus Christ.

Hebrews 13:2 Be not forgetful to entertain strangers: for thereby some have entertained angels unawares.

If we read our bible carefully and take what we read seriously we are told that there is a war going on all around us. A war that has been continually fought since long before any of us were born. What I find most interesting of all regarding this eternal conflict is how blissfully unaware we remain.

Where to begin, that is the question. There is so much that can be said regarding this subject, yet there is the temptation to give it short shrift at the same time when it is something one grew up with it doesn't seem to have the importance others may place on it. It appears to be common. One might say no one is interested in all that, everybody already knows, but that isn't really the truth now is it. The title came to mind after discussing a preview for a video I had seen on line with

The Great Deception of the Mandela Effect

my sister. I knew she is a fan of the documentarian so I thought if anyone has this video, she does. So I gave her a call. Nope, she didn't have it but my older sister did and she gave it to her daughter, but her daughter didn't like it. I wasn't surprised by this as the video was all about other dimensional entities. Spooky stuff if you ask me. I wanted to see it, as I write this I still want to see it, and I will one of these days. Considering this documentary and my niece's reaction to it there is no surprise there. She has had a long fascination with the supernatural so one might think this would be a film she would be naturally interested in, but not exposes the lies of the multidimensional beings. There is the rub! The scripture passage reminding us that some have entertained angels unawares came to mind, and that inspired me to begin this modest project.

Entertaining demons is exactly what many do when they delve into the supernatural when they give in to new age temptations when they give ear to the lie. What lie? You might ask, the first lie, the same lie that humans have listened to and fallen prey to from the very beginning, the lie Satan told Eve in the garden of Eden, that knowing good and

The Great Deception of the Mandela Effect

evil she would be like God! Eve willingly gives ear to this lie, and every day somewhere someone listens to the self-same lie and chooses to believe it. Why? Because they want to! They want to be special, they want to know things no one else knows, they want to have power no one else has, why do they listen? In one word the answer is pride. Pride the first sin, the fault that was found in Lucifer that ultimately was his downfall is at the heart of what he has to sell in his lies still today.

How so? What on earth are you talking about? You might ask. Be patient with me and you will see for yourself exactly what I am talking about. In this area, I speak from experience. I know of what I speak. So bare with me and let me unburden my soul.

My family has a history of delving into this realm. I don't know with what generation it began, but I do know it was well settled in with my maternal grandparents. Anna was my mother's stepmother. Anna had some familiar ties to some petty German nobility, I never quite understood where or how but she did mention relatives who had footmen and such before the war. The war in question is, of course, the

The Great Deception of the Mandela Effect

great war, the war to end all wars, WW1, which of course you will recall was soon followed by WW2, and then Korea, and Viet Nam, and so on and so forth. So much for ending all wars. But does lend a certain naiveté a certain innocence to the generation of my grandparents, that appears to have been replaced by cynicism in my own generation.

When one carefully thinks about the history of the world and more recently the history of the twentieth-century one can see the effects of the celestial war acted out on the human stage. The Great War set the stage for World War Two where the Nazis in an effort to gain control of the world in preparation for the coming of the Antichrist. They also conducted a savage campaign to exterminate God's chosen people. The Nazi's allied themselves with the Muslim nations that were all too willing to help anyone attempting genocide against the Jews. The allied forces eventually won the victory over the Nazis in Europe stopping the bloodshed for a time, but the Nazi sympathizers in the west and in high places in the United States were still there in places of power waiting, biding their time until they found the opportunity to try again. The battle never stopped entirely

The Great Deception of the Mandela Effect

the war continued in Korea, and then in Viet Nam. In these conflicts, we can see the spiritual war that has continued from the time Satan was cast out of Heaven played out on earth with human players. In world war two the Axis and their secret allies in the west fought fiercely to exterminate God's chosen people from the face of the earth while at the same time fighting to prepare the earth for a one world government in preparation for the arrival of the Antichrist. In Korea and Viet Nam, we can see the communists doing their best to defeat and kill the Christians residing in the bordering capitalist nations. During the 1990's the United States government took the side of the Muslims in their Jihad against the Christians in what was once Yugoslavia. The United States took part in genocide helping the Muslims kill Christians by the millions. Currently, The war can be seen not only in the middle east where rampant persecution not seen since the days of Caligula is taking place while the Muslims supported again by the United States are driving those Christian fortunate enough to survive their barbarity are forced out of their homes and countries. But this battle isn't limited to the middle east it has spilled out into Europe

The Great Deception of the Mandela Effect

with the influx of jihadis coming in under the guise of being refugees from the many conflicts in the middle east. Once in their host nation, they riot and destroy the peace bringing chaos in their wake. You may say all right there have been wars throughout the last century through to today and perhaps wars throughout human history, there is nothing new here, nothing remarkable at all. That it isn't remarkable in itself shows what a sad state of affairs we have grown comfortable living within.

Political and physical conflict are only the basest ways this ancient war can be perceived. In truth, this conflict is spiritual at its roots, therefore, we must look a little deeper into the matter.

The Great Deception of the Mandela Effect

The Great Deception of the Mandela Effect

Chapter Seven

*S*o we find ourselves, pawns, in the middle of a spiritual war that has been going on since time immemorial, in a realty that seems to have lost its own sense of balance, perhaps it would be a good idea for us to take a look at who exactly our enemies are.

"For if God spared not angels when they sinned, but cast them down to hell, and committed them to pits of darkness, to be reserved unto judgment;" II Peter 2:4

Prior to his fall from heaven, Lucifer was the name given to Satan. He was the Shining one, the Morning Star, But that was not to last. The bible indicates that it was Lucifer's pride that inspired his rebellion against God. It was his pride that inspired his ill-fated attempt at overthrowing the throne of God. Tradition has it that shortly after the creation of man, in God's image and likeness, Lucifer rebelled at the thought of angels serving an inferior creature than themselves. When

The Great Deception of the Mandela Effect

God told his angels that they were to minister to mankind Lucifer refused and with a third of the angels of heaven following him rebelled against God. Lucifer was cast out of Heaven, he was no longer The morning Star, but Satan the accuser, the enemy of God, the lord of evil, and the tempter and adversary of human beings.

In the past, Satan has been depicted as a cute little red devil with horns, a little shiny red pitchfork, and a pointed tail in comics and cartoons longer than anyone living today can remember. This trend began sometime in the middle ages as an attempt to ridicule the devil where it would hurt him the most, his pride. However, there is no biblical evidence to suggest that this description is in any way accurate. In fact, Satan as a little red devil is about as accurate a description of Lucifer as chubby little babies with wings and bows and arrows is of the cherubim surrounding God's throne.

The bible describes Satan as being radiantly beautiful. We find God at first discussing the King of Tyre, but soon is describing the Prince, the supernatural power behind the throne of the kingdom of Tyre, that is Satan. In Ezekiel 28:12-15 it reads "Thus saith the Lord Jehovah: Thou sealest up the sum, full of wisdom, and perfect in beauty. Thou wast in Eden, the garden of God; every precious stone was thy covering, the sardius, the topaz, and the diamond, the beryl, the onyx, and the jasper, the sapphire, the emerald, and the carbuncle, and gold: the workmanship of thy tabrets and of thy pipes was in thee; in the day that thou wast created they were prepared. Thou wast the anointed cherub that covereth: and I set thee, so that, thou wast upon the holy mountain of God; thou hast walked up and down in the midst of the stones of fire. Thou wast perfect in thy ways from the day that thou wast created, till unrighteousness was found in thee."

The bible states it was ultimately because of Satan's pride in his beauty that he was cast down from heaven. It is recorded in Ezekiel 28:17 "Thy heart was lifted up because of thy beauty; thou hast corrupted thy wisdom by reason of thy brightness: I have cast thee to the ground; I have laid thee before kings, that they may behold thee"

In Isaiah 14:12-15 it reads concerning Lucifer, "How are you fallen from heaven, O Lucifer, son of the morning! How are you cut down to the ground, which did weaken the nations!

The Great Deception of the Mandela Effect

For you have said in your heart, I will ascend into heaven, I will exalt my throne above the stars of God: I will sit also upon the mount of the congregation, in the sides of the north: I will ascend above the heights of the clouds; I will be like the most High. Yet you shall be brought down to hell, to the sides of the pit."

From what is written in the book of genesis we cannot tell how long mankind lived in the garden of Eden before falling into temptation, was it a day or a thousand years? We have no way of knowing. What we do know is that Satan tempted our ancestors with the lie that if we disobeyed God and ate of the tree of the knowledge of good and evil we would become as gods, knowing both good and evil. It didn't quite work out as we were led to believe, now did it? We died spiritually, we were no longer physically immortal, we lost dominion over the world by handing that over to Satan and we were cursed by God. Genesis 1:16- 19 describes it thus "Unto the woman he said, I will greatly multiply thy pain and thy conception; in pain, thou shalt bring forth children; and thy desire shall be to thy husband, and he shall rule over thee. And unto Adam he said, Because thou hast hearkened

The Great Deception of the Mandela Effect

unto the voice of thy wife, and hast eaten of the tree, of which I commanded thee, saying, Thou shalt not eat of it: cursed is the ground for thy sake; in toil shalt thou eat of it all the days of thy life; thorns also and thistles shall it bring forth to thee; and thou shalt eat the herb of the field; in the sweat of thy face shalt thou eat bread, till thou return unto the ground; for out of it wast thou taken: for dust thou art, and unto dust shalt thou return."

This certainly changes our status in the world, but we were not left without hope for as God spoke Satan's punishment into being He also allowed us a glimmer of hope for in Genesis 1:14-15 it reads "And Jehovah God said unto the serpent, Because thou hast done this, cursed art thou above all cattle, and above every beast of the field; upon thy belly shalt thou go, and dust shalt thou eat all the days of thy life: and I will put enmity between thee and the woman, and between thy seed and her seed: he shall bruise thy head, and thou shalt bruise his heel." The glimmer of hope comes from the final sentence in the passage above. Remember God spoke the universe into existence, what he speaks comes to pass. By saying the woman's seed will bruise the serpents

The Great Deception of the Mandela Effect

head God is in effect promising a Savior to come from the seed of the woman. A champion who will strike a fatal blow against our ancient enemy Satan.

From that moment on Satan has been acutely aware of the coming of a champion for mankind, a champion who will strike a fatal blow to his head. We know that champion as Jesus the Christ. Did Satan idly accept his coming fate? No, he laid plans to subvert the coming of the Christ and he wasted no time in putting those plans into action.

Genesis 6:2 reads "that the sons of God saw the daughters of men that they were fair, and they took them wives of all that they chose." First of all, who are these sons of God? In the Old Testament the phrase "sons of god" always refers to angels. So we have angels leaving heaven to mate with the daughters of men. If we read further we see that the offspring of these unions are giants. Reading Genesis 6:4 we see that "The Nephilim were on the earth in those days, and also after that, when the sons of God came in unto the daughters of men, and they bare children to them: the same were the mighty men that were of old, the men of renown." The Nephilim are the offspring of the fallen angels and

The Great Deception of the Mandela Effect

human women. The word Nephilim in the original Hebrew means "the fallen ones" In the Septuagint bible the word Nephilim was transliterated as the word giants, but the Greek word used actually means "Earth born"

What was the point of this? Why did these angels desire to interbreed with humans? Did they really see human women as irresistible, so irresistible in fact that they left their own habitation that is heaven to mate with them? I propose that the purpose of this interbreeding was to pollute the human gene pool thereby preventing the possibility of Christ being born of the seed of the woman. Genesis 6:6-7 tells us God's reaction to this interbreeding. "And it repented Jehovah that he had made a man on the earth, and it grieved him at his heart. And Jehovah said, I will destroy man whom I have created from the face of the ground; both man, and beast, and creeping things, and birds of the heavens; for it repenteth me that I have made them." So God took this act of rebellion so seriously that he was going to destroy everything thing on the planet, but then he took note of Noah, who was perfect in all his generations. That is to say,

The Great Deception of the Mandela Effect

he was genetically pure, in all his generations, undefiled, by the rebellious angel's efforts.

Regarding the fate of those angels who chose to interbreed with humans Jude 1:6-7 states. "And angels that kept not their own principality, but left their proper habitation, he hath kept in everlasting bonds under darkness unto the judgment of the great day. Even as Sodom and Gomorrah, and the cities about them, having in like manner with these given themselves over to fornication and gone after strange flesh, are set forth as an example, suffering the punishment of eternal fire."

To bring this chapter to a close let me conclude that Lucifer's pride motivated him to rebel against God in an attempt to overthrow the throne of God. That Saint Michael and the heavenly host composed of those angels who remained loyal to God cast Lucifer out of heaven to the Earth.

Upon the Earth, Lucifer no longer the shining one, now know as Satan or the accuser, tempted mankind with the thought of becoming like God, knowing both good and evil. Mankind with Satan was then punished by God and cast out of Eden, the way back blocked by mighty cherubim. Even in punishing mankind, the way of redemption was foretold in the phrase "I will put enmity between thee and the woman, and between thy seed and her seed: he shall bruise thy head, and thou shalt bruise his heel." thereby, giving mankind hope of redemption and Satan a warning that the humans would have a champion coming from the seed of the woman. To prevent this champion from ever coming into existence Satan encouraged some of his followers to interbreed with humans thereby corrupting the human gene pool making it an unfit route for the appearance of the Messiah. God found a man with an undefiled genetic heritage and decided to cleanse the earth from all corruption with a global flood while saving that single uncorrupted specimen of human DNA. Confirming this is Genesis 6:9-13 which states "These are the generations of Noah. Noah was a righteous man, and perfect in his generations: Noah walked with God. And Noah begat three sons, Shem, Ham, and Japheth. And the earth was corrupt before God, and the earth was filled with violence. And God saw the earth, and, behold, it was corrupt; for all flesh had corrupted their way upon the earth. And God said unto Noah, The end of all flesh is come before

The Great Deception of the Mandela Effect

me; for the earth is filled with violence through them; and, behold, I will destroy them with the earth."

Following this passage is the record of the flood destroying all the flesh from the earth except Noah, his family, and the creatures saved on the arc. This drastic action temporarily cleansed the earth from corruption and provided an undefiled genetic line from which the Messiah would arise.

A word about demons, many people believe demon is just another word for fallen angel. It sounds like it makes sense, Satan's name was changed when he fell, why not the name of the fallen angels as well? But demon is not an individual's name as Lucifer or Satan is, Demon is a class or perhaps more specifically a hybrid between two created species, much as a mule is the offspring of a male donkey and a female horse, a demon is the spirit that remains after physical death of one of the Nephilim. Fallen angels remain angels after their fall. They retain the characteristics of angels and the abilities of angels. They may have lost their place in heaven, but they remain angels nonetheless. Nephilim, on the other hand, are the hybrid offspring of the fallen angels discussed in the sixth chapter of Genesis and in

The Great Deception of the Mandela Effect

the book of Enoch. They are the mighty men of old, the demigods of the pagans, the giants of the past. They are neither angel nor are they human. The Nephilim are the result of Satan's attempt to thwart Gods plan of redemption for mankind by corrupting the human gene pool. This plan failed. God saved a genetically undefiled sample of the genetic code by saving Noah and his family from the global flood.

The Nephilim alive at the time of the flood presumably drowned in the flood. But what of their spirits? Do they go to heaven? Do they go to hell? They roam the earth seeking whom they may inhabit.

You might ask how are demons and fallen angels different? First and perhaps most importantly fallen angels are a direct creation of God just as Adam was. Demons were sired of fallen angels and born of human women. Angels were created spiritual beings and will not die, demons were born of human women as Nephilim and have already died. They now roam the earth as demons. Fallen angels can cloth themselves in flesh. They can appear to us as human beings, as angels of light, or remain invisible to us as they desire.

The Great Deception of the Mandela Effect

Demons cannot cloth themselves in flesh unless they take possession of and occupy the flesh of a human.

As a born again Christian you are indwelt by the Holy Spirit and cannot be possessed by a demon, but you can be oppressed. The Holy Spirit within you allows no room for a demon to enter in, that is unless by invitation. Who would be foolish enough to invite a demon into their own body? Well, first of all, it doesn't have to be a formal invitation. You don't need to go to a crossroads at midnight to make a deal with the devil or try your hand at mediumship nothing as dramatic as that is necessary to open yourself up to demonic influences. What would do it then, you ask. A few activities come to mind right away, such as listening to psychics, or fortune tellers, going to mediums attending a séance, chanting mantras, listening to music or watching movies glorifying Satan or violence, and drug abuse to name a few. You may say I only listen to that because I like the beat, or those movies are exciting, but I'm not inviting any demons in when I watch, or I only went to see the psychic to see if my boyfriend is the right one. It's all just in fun, nothing serious. The thing is although it only fun and games to you it is all

The Great Deception of the Mandela Effect

the opportunity some demon needs to reach in and gain as a toehold in your soul. Don't think I'm saying that overnight you change from an innocent babe in the woods to the poor child depicted in the movie "the Exorcist" because you listened to some violent rap lyrics, or because you read your horoscope in the morning newspaper. No, but you did open the door a crack, and a crack is enough for a demon to get your ear, and once it has your ear it won't be too long before it begins oppressing you with unwanted thoughts and temptations designed to lead you to open the door wider.

Now that we have discussed the differences between angels, fallen angels, and demons let us spend a little effort exploring the many ways we may be entertaining demons unawares.

My family has a history of being involved in the occult. I can't claim to know how far back this interest goes. I haven't attempted to do a spiritual genealogy or anything of that kind although it may prove to be interesting if I did. The point I am trying to make is simply that I am no stranger to the supernatural. My mother's stepmother Anna, was a practicing medium. Not the kind that put themselves out for

The Great Deception of the Mandela Effect

hire and was, therefore, prone to fraud to keep their audiences satisfied, but the more independent type that did what they did for their own purposes. My mother, of course, grew up under her influence and was made aware of the existence of an immaterial world beyond our own from a very early age. What my mother may have experienced in her childhood and youth I do not claim to know, but I do know of her interest in the supernatural and the occult during my own childhood.

I recall certain occurrences in our home at the top of Blanchard hill when I was a child. I remember being visited by a shadowy figure of a woman dressed in a black floor-length dress with a bustle on more than one occasion. The figure would pass through my bedroom pausing for a moment here or there as if it had found something of interest and then it would be gone. When I was about six years old I had a toy xylophone that I kept on my dresser, on those rare occasions when I tried to keep my room in order, now and then it would play a few discordant notes from what appeared to be its own accord. Now that I write this I remember Anna saying after my grandfather had died that

The Great Deception of the Mandela Effect

she would know that he was visiting her when the wind chimes she kept indoors would begin to play.

My parents were given a print of the "Blue Boy" that my grandparents had kept in their home for many years. My mother hung the painting in the master bedroom. From that moment on, our pet dog, Fancy, was terrified of my parent's bedroom and would not enter of its own free will. If Fancy was carried into the room she would run out as fast as her short little legs would carry her as soon as it was free to do so. I believe something inherently unfriendly entered the master bedroom along with the print of the "Blue Boy".

For a time, my mother, sisters and I would play with an Ouija board on a fairly regular basis. It was exciting to think that we were communicating with an unseen spirit. I remember us children hunting for treasure hidden somewhere in the basement under the Ouija board's direction. There was a game of my mother's invention where she would place colored pick up sticks in a brown paper bag and us children would take turns reaching in, touch a pick up stick, and then try to feel or sense what color it was by the warmth or coolness we felt in the stick before bringing it out

The Great Deception of the Mandela Effect

of the bag. I recall quite clearly being told to try to feel the warmth of the color. As time passed and we grew older the games changed. Instead of using colored pick up sticks we would use a deck of playing cards and try to predict first whether the card was a face card or a number card, then the color, and then the suit before we looked at the card in our hand.

By the time I was a teenager, my mother was involved in an organization called the "Chicago Psychic Society" led by Doctor Clifford Royce. Attending classes at the Chicago Psychic Society was a fairly common weekend activity for my mother and oldest sister. I rarely, if ever attended, but not because of a lack of interest, only a lack of funds. On one occasion we traveled to the city to see a guru of one sort or another, my mother and sister went in to meet with him and be given their own personal mantra, I waited in the car. At the time I felt left out, but today, I am glad I didn't attend that meeting. I had one less piece of spiritual baggage to get rid of thanks to waiting in the car.

Don't think that I didn't act to advance my own interests regarding the occult. I may not have had the money to attend

The Great Deception of the Mandela Effect

lectures at the Chicago Psychic Society but I did find enough money to join the Theosophical Society. As a member at large, I had the privilege of borrowing books from the library at their national headquarters in Wheaton Illinois. This was the most complete library of the occult and supernatural I would ever find. I made a habit of visiting the library and on occasion, I would attend lectures and meetings held at the National Headquarters building. Whenever we, as a family, would get together, we would spend time practicing our psychic abilities, giving each other readings through psychometry or other means attempting to hone our skills to a razor's edge. Individually, we would meditate attempting to clear our minds to be ever more open to the influences of the supernatural. This we hoped would increase our psychic abilities. For a time my oldest sister and I experimented in astral travel. I remember on one such occasion, my sister and I decided to try an experiment in astral travel where we could have some objective feedback other than relying on what the traveler claimed to experience afterward. At the time I was a teenager living with my mother in an apartment building, one of my sisters lived in

The Great Deception of the Mandela Effect

the same apartment complex a few units down from us. For this experiment, I left my sister's apartment and went to my bedroom to my mother's apartment. My oldest sister was to attempt to free her spirit and travel immaterially from our sister's home to mine. I was to be the receiver, so to speak, to wait and perceive whatever I could during a given period of time. I lay quietly on my bed meditating, trying to free my mind from any distractions, waiting to see whatever I might see.

At the same time, my sister attempted to travel to my room from our sister's apartment. After only a few moments waiting I saw, entering my room, not my sister, but what appeared to be a wet grayish white cloud of ectoplasm. It entered through the bedroom door crossed across the room in front of my bed and approached me. I had read about ectoplasm but had never seen it before this. I panicked, I waved my arms in front of myself, trying to signal it to get away from me, it kept coming. I jumped over my bed in order to get out of my room without getting any closer to the grayish mass floating in my room than I absolutely had to. I ran straight to my sister's apartment. No sooner than I got in

The Great Deception of the Mandela Effect

the door than my sister approached me and asking what the hand waving meant. She saw me! She thought I was trying to signal her! What did my hand waving mean? My hand-waving meant I was scared silly and couldn't wait to get out of there. Of course, as far as astral projection was concerned we considered the experiment a success.

When I was young I continued to seek out experiences of a mystical or supernatural nature. I came by this interest with my mother's encouragement. We experimented with extrasensory perception, various arcane arts, and practices such as astrology, tarot card reading, psychometry, psychic photography, and even mediumship. It was not uncommon to ask each other for psychic readings at family gatherings. I remember setting up a system in attempting to make psychic recordings. I was very careful to block out any ambient noise so that whatever I managed to record would have no natural explanation. I don't recall the results of this effort. I do recall after learning that mediums would meditate in a cabinet in the attempt to bring about physical manifestations that I cleared out a closet, placed a chair inside and tried it myself. While I was meditating in the closet, my mother was sitting

The Great Deception of the Mandela Effect

in the room observing. Was sixteen or seventeen t the time and styled myself as a hippie, my hair was shoulder length. After awhile of meditating in silence I felt something near my side and then a clump of my hair was lifted up as if someone lifted it between their thumb and forefinger. I felt it, my mother witnessed it, and I got out of the makeshift cabinet as fast as I could. One would think that a fright like that would discourage me from any further experiments, on the contrary, it only encouraged me all the more. I would meditate, attempting to empty my mind from any distractions, any thoughts in order to open myself up to the spirit world. I thought I was being oh so spiritual.

Over time my efforts were rewarded and I would frequently see lavender sparklers filling my room. I would see them clearest in the dark. I came to think of them as spiritual background noise. Later I would think of them as an indication of how spiritual a person was. I remember when I was still in the air force a friend of mine was house sitting for a Catholic chaplain and he invited me over. I saw lavender sparklers engulfing the priest's house and rise to

The Great Deception of the Mandela Effect

the sky. This convinced me that the sparklers were more than spiritual background noise.

I would practice my breathing and relaxation techniques reciting generic mantra at night hoping to make myself so much more in tune with the spiritual ether. I would empty my mind as much as I could opening myself up to whatever may come, thinking that for it to be spiritual it must be good. I recall that on many occasion the sparklers I came to see on a regular basis when ever the lights were dim enough not to outshine them would begin to swirl much as galaxies swirl about their center black hole. I suspected that these whirly-gigs as I called them were spirits from a higher plan attempting to communicate with me. One night one such whirly-gig formed at the foot of my bed at about head height. I focused my attention on it, watching attentively until a face, then a complete head of a swarthy man wearing a turban formed. You would think that I would be overjoyed with this event. After all, this appearance in and of itself was not frightening, but the feeling of dread that accompanied it was terrifying. I ran out of my room and when I did venture back in I am sure I left the lights on for the remainder of the

The Great Deception of the Mandela Effect

night. A similar experience occurred one night. It began as a dream. In the dream I was observing a multitude of people burning in a valley, that must have been hell. They were burning, but they were not being consumed by the flames. This vision woke me with a start and when I opened my eyes there sitting at the foot of my bed was my long deceased grandfather. This frightened me more than the dream. Looking back, I suspect this may have been an instance where I was being warned away from the path I was currently following, not that I was mature enough to heed the warning. I didn't lose my interest in the supernatural, but I gave up meditation and any exercises designed to heighten my perception. The blue sparklers were more than enough for me now.

You might ask if any of our experiments and interest in the supernatural affected our lives in any way. Of course, it did. My youngest sister had the unpleasant experience of sharing her home with a poltergeist. The lights would come on and go off at their own discretion, vegetables would move in their bags, the dish drainer was thrown off of the kitchen counter to land somehow squeezed on its side between the

The Great Deception of the Mandela Effect

sink and the stove, and doors would open and close on their own.

I am ashamed to admit that I thought this was the perfect opportunity to dabble a little deeper into the occult and convinced my brother-in-law to go along with me in attempting necromancy. Against my sister's wishes, I drew a pentagram using her lipstick on the living room floor followed the directions given in a book of black magic I had purchased and brought to her home. I recited the invocation provided in the book and nothing happened. Nothing happened that night at least as far as we could tell other than making a mess and wasting a tube of lipstick. In time it became clear that this little experiment had the same effect as pouring gasoline on a fire.

The poltergeist activity increased rather than decreased. The height of the paranormal activity came during the holiday season. The Christmas tree was up and beautifully decorated. We were all looking forward to Christmas, but the poltergeist would not leave the tree alone. Ornaments would fly from the tree and across the room. At one point the Christmas tree was rocking so violently back and forth

The Great Deception of the Mandela Effect

that it was throwing multiple ornaments off the tree and across the room.

Although I was present during some of the poltergeist activity, I wasn't present when the tree was rocking. This did, however, affect me years later when my mother gave me a picture in a black frame that my sister had previously owned, I hung it in the living room. The following Christmas season, by this time I had become at least a nominal Christian, we placed our tree next to the wall perpendicular to the wall where the picture hung. After the tree was up and decorated with lights and ornaments the picture frame began to move rocking back and forth slightly, but noticeably while still hanging on the wall.

I approached for a closer look and in the reflection, in the glass, I saw our Christmas tree rocking back and forth. I looked from the picture to the tree and the tree was still. I looked back to the picture and the reflection of the tree continued rocking violently. The frame itself was rocking side to side. I knew enough by then not to allow that to stay in my home any longer. I took the picture and frame out and

The Great Deception of the Mandela Effect

threw it in the trash. We had no further experience with the tree or pictures on the wall.

It was in this home where I had what may have been an experience with an angel. At the time my young wife was pregnant with my oldest daughter, Melissa. I would frequently walk to the local convenience store as the apartment building was only a couple of buildings away. I would go there on errands for my wife. I made many trips there to buy a hot spicy dill pickle and a pint of Haagen-Dazs ice cream to soothe my wife's cravings. This occurred on a trip such as this whether it was on a trip to buy a pickle or some other errand, I don't remember, but what happened on the way I remember quite clearly. You see there was a little hill between the last house and the convenience store and this hill was made higher with plowed snow from the store's parking lot. I being relatively young at the time, would climb over this icy hill rather than taking the safer route and walk in the street. This night I climbed the hill and once at the top started to fall backward and was falling to the hard ice covered asphalt behind me when suddenly I felt a large hand pressed against my back at my shoulder blades. It

The Great Deception of the Mandela Effect

felt as if someone reached down to me to stop my fall like a father would to steady his little boy. This unseen hand touched my back at my shoulder blades and stopped my fall. I could very clearly feel the hand as it pressed into my back, the fingers were pointing down towards the ground so it was literally as if a father reached down to steady his falling son. But you see I was fully grown and six feet one inch tall, who ever reached down to steady me had to be much taller than me. There was no one visible there to prevent my fall or to have helped me in any way.

That one experience so many years ago began my seriously thinking of angels. The experience brings to mind the 91st Psalm which states "For he will give his angels charge over thee, To keep thee in all thy ways. They shall bear thee up in their hands, Lest thou dash thy foot against a stone." or in my case crack my head against the icy asphalt.

I should make a point of explaining one more thing. Although I am certain we considered ourselves Christians when I was a child, we were not. We did not go to church except on very rare occasions. We did, however, celebrate the secular holidays. On Halloween my sister and I would

The Great Deception of the Mandela Effect

dress up and go trick-or-treating, on Thanksgiving we would visit family and eat turkey, on Christmas we would open presents, and on New Year's eve we would stay up late and make noise. We celebrated the holidays with a fairly shallow depth of faith.

I did not become a Christian overnight. While I was serving in the Air Force an acquaintance of mine decided he would invest his time and money witnessing to me. He wanted me to hear Christian tapes from a certain pastor who had once been an Air Force Chaplain, so he offered me the tapes. I had little interest and no tape player so I declined his offer; so he gave me a reel to reel tape recorder to play the tapes on. He spent time explaining his understanding of the bible to me and I would share my understanding spiritualism and eastern meditation with him. I would like to say he convinced me and I was born again then and there, but that didn't happen for a number of years. What Roger Moore, (not the actor) did do was plant the seeds that would mature and eventually lead me to Christ. The day I was finally convinced of the truth by reading the Confessions of Saint Augustine, I decide to become a Christian. I sought out and

The Great Deception of the Mandela Effect

found a priest willing to instruct me and later that year, I, my four-year-old son, and my father were baptized at Saint Joan of Arc Church in Lisle Illinois. My life changed after that and continues to change day by day to this day.

Years passed. I fulfilled my commitment to the military and following a rather serpentine path found myself occupied in a career as a psychiatric technician, then a psychiatric counselor. My duties were varied and for the most part interesting. I first worked in a suburban hospital and was advised that most of the patients I would meet would be bored housewives and delinquent teens. For some time that proved to be true, however in the years that followed things changed. In the mid to late 1980's several victims of ritual crimes were admitted to the psychiatric unit where I was employed. More teens than adult victims, but there were adults who had been ritually abused as children and who had been forced to take part and or lure children away to be victimized.

The Great Deception of the Mandela Effect

Chapter Eight

"*B*lessed be the Lord, my rock, who trains my hands for war, and my fingers for battle; He is my steadfast love and my fortress, my stronghold and my deliverer, my shield and he in whom I take refuge, who subdues peoples under me."
-Psalm 144:1, 2

In jest, my wife once threatened to open a can of whoop-ass on me, or one of our children, I don't clearly remember which, but the phrase has stayed with me until today when I am borrowing it for the heading to this chapter discussing spiritual warfare. What exactly is meant by spiritual warfare? Are ghosts arming up and plotting an invasion into the physical realm in which we live? Not exactly. Saint Paul tells us in II Corinthians 10:3-5 "For though we walk in the flesh, we do not war according to the flesh (for the weapons of our warfare are not of the flesh, but mighty before God to the casting down of strongholds), casting down imaginations, and every high thing that is exalted against the

The Great Deception of the Mandela Effect

knowledge of God, and bringing every thought into captivity to the obedience of Christ;" According to this passage we are battling against thoughts and imaginations that are counter to the knowledge of God. This truly is spiritual combat within our own minds, but is that all there is to it?

Saint Paul tells us that there is more to spiritual warfare than our controlling our own thoughts and emotions in Ephesians 6:12 "For our wrestling is not against flesh and blood, but against the principalities, against the powers, against the world-rulers of this darkness, against the spiritual hosts of wickedness in the heavenly places" When Paul is talking about Principalities and powers he is talking about the hierarchy of angels. We are pawns in the middle of the spiritual war that began before recorded human history when Lucifer let his pride get the better of him and he attempted a rebellion against God. Revelation 12:7- tells us "And there was war in heaven: Michael and his angels going forth to war with the dragon; and the dragon warred and his angels; And they prevailed not, neither was their place found any more in heaven. And the great dragon was cast down, the old serpent, he that is called the Devil and Satan, the deceiver of

The Great Deception of the Mandela Effect

the whole world; he was cast down to the earth, and his angels were cast down with him." Lucifer no longer the morning star, now has become Satan the snake who was introduced to our first ancestors in Eden. Where he successfully tempted us into joining his rebellion against God with the offer of becoming like God knowing both good and evil. If only our first parents remembered who they were, for they were already created in the image and likeness of God. They were like God already, enough like God for Satan vent his hatred against God on them. Satan through deceit stole mankind's place in creation, stole the dominion God had given mankind over the Earth. Don't doubt that this skirmish in the celestial war had long lasting effects. Remember from the previous chapter when God punished mankind and Satan for their disobedience He promised a champion to restore mankind. Satan has from that time on fought to prevent God's will for mankind from being realized.

We were born in the midst of this war, it is all we have ever known. We are so used to it that many of us remain unaware of it even though it is going all around us. We are oblivious

The Great Deception of the Mandela Effect

to its spiritual origins, we are blind to the other dimensional aspects of battles that effect out day to day lives. But what does the bible have to tell us about this war? In II Corinthians 10:3 it reads "For though we walk in the flesh, we do not war according to the flesh." In Ephesians 6:12 it states "For our wrestling is not against flesh and blood, but against the principalities, against the powers, against the world-rulers of this darkness, against the spiritual hosts of wickedness in the heavenly places." From these two passages we see that not only do we walk in the flesh, but that our enemies do not, our enemies are high ranking spiritual beings principalities and powers. Furthermore, I Peter 5:8 warns us to "Be sober, be watchful: your adversary the devil, as a roaring lion, walketh about, seeking whom he may devour". Many of us do not believe there is a real devil. It is not politically correct to think that there is a personification of evil out there roaming about seeking whom he may destroy, but the bible tells us otherwise. How are we to cope with this state of affairs? Saint Paul tells us in Ephesians 6:13-18 "Wherefore take up the whole armor of God, that ye may be able to withstand in the evil

The Great Deception of the Mandela Effect

day, and, having done all, to stand. Stand therefore, having girded your loins with truth, and having put on the breastplate of righteousness, and having shod your feet with the preparation of the gospel of peace; withal taking up the shield of faith, wherewith ye shall be able to quench all the fiery darts of the evil one. And take the helmet of salvation, and the sword of the Spirit, which is the word of God: with all prayer and supplication praying at all seasons in the Spirit, and watching thereunto in all perseverance and supplication for all the saints,"

Saint Paul reminds us we have not been left defenseless. We in fact have been commanded to take up our armor and to defend ourselves. We are to prepare ourselves with the Truth that is that Christ has paid the price for our sins. We are to put on the breastplate of righteousness. How are we supposed to do that you ask? What is righteousness? How does one become righteous? Righteousness first of all is right standing with God. By our own efforts it is impossible to become righteous, but Christ has paid the price for our sins by dying in our place on the cross and we can put on His righteousness by confessing our sins to God who is then

The Great Deception of the Mandela Effect

faithful and just in forgiving us our sins, thereby making us righteous. We are then to prepare ourselves with the gospel of peace, and take up the shield of faith. How then are we to do this? Simply by studying God's word, the bible. We are to wear the helmet of salvation and carry the sword of the Spirit, which is the word of God and last we are to pray in all seasons in the Spirit and in all perseverance and supplications for all the saints, that is our brothers and sisters in Christ.

How can we expect to be attacked personally? Just as Christ was attacked before us. He was tempted by our adversary Satan and our Lord responded by quoting scripture. Until we can quote scripture as well as out Lord. I suggest we take a hint from the prayer attributed to Saint Francis quoted below.

"Lord, make us instruments of your peace. Where there is hatred, let us sow love; where there is injury, pardon; where there is discord, union; where there is doubt, faith; where there is despair, hope; where there is darkness, light; where there is sadness, joy. Grant that we may not so much seek to be consoled as to console; to be understood as to understand;

to be loved as to love. For it is in giving that we receive; it is in pardoning that we are pardoned; and it is in dying that we are born to eternal life. Amen."

Do you notice a pattern in this beautiful prayer? There is a pattern of opposites contained in this prayer. When tempted to hate, sow love; when tempted to unforgivingness, sow forgiveness; when tempted to argue, restore the peace, when tempted to doubt, respond with faith in Christ, when tempted to despair respond with hope in Christ; and when there is spiritual darkness you are to be the reflected light of Christ. I'm sure you get the idea. We are not to passively succumb to temptation, but are to resist the devil as it says in James 4:7 "Be subject therefore unto God; but resist the devil, and he will flee from you."

Finally, we are not to forget the big guns available to us, prayer. It was the prayers of the local church which prompted God to send one of His angels to free Peter from prison. Prayer is like calling in an air strike against our enemy, it is calling on our allies the angels to come to our aid and rescue. Remember James 5:16 "Confess therefore your sins one to another, and pray one for another, that ye

The Great Deception of the Mandela Effect

may be healed. The supplication of a righteous man availeth much in its working" Confessing your sins brings you back into a state of righteousness, or right standing with God, and the prayers of the righteous avail much.

Chapter Nine
The Great Deception

When we talk about the great deception, what exactly are we talking about? Are the changes observed by those aware of the Mandela effect deception in and of themselves? Or is this simply preparing the soil by means of cognitive dissonance for even greater deception. Sowing doubt in the minds of Christians by distorting verses in the bible, while at the same time opening their minds to the ancient lies of the new age movement. Is the Mandela Effect preparing the soil of ignorance to accept the seeds of the Antichrist?

The deception is not limited to Mandela Effect changes in the bible, nor to secular cultural changes in movie dialogue or brand logos. The deception runs deeper than that. It includes false teaching within the church. The church has bent over backwards attempting to please the world. Sin is no longer called sin, but rather an alternative lifestyle. Many churches preach a gospel of acquiring worldly wealth and in

The Great Deception of the Mandela Effect

effect have made money riches their god. Yet, that appears to be what the congregation seeks as they come back week after week to listen to another sermon on how giving money to the church will make them rich. These churches look at God as great vending machine in the sky! Donate enough that the pastor can buy a new plane, or add an addition to his pet's air conditioned dog house and god will give you the desires of your heart. Somewhere these pastors have forgotten Christ's command to take up your cross and follow me! At one time the United States could be considered a Christian nation as could most of the nations of Europe, but not today. The stench of apostasy reeks throughout the land. The mega churches may be full, the liberal churches may draw a crowd with their clown services, but the number of Christians in this world is much smaller than you may suspect. The papacy along with many of the popular mega churches is promoting chrislam, an obscene melding of Christianity with Islam. I can't help but ask, how does one combine Islam with Christianity when Islam is actively murdering Christians by decapitation, or burning them alive for refusing to deny Christ. Most recently Members of the

The Great Deception of the Mandela Effect

Islamic cult ISIS have claimed credit for bombing two Coptic churches during their Palm Sunday worship services killing hundreds, yet Pope Francis says there is no difference between the church and Islam. Could it be he too is laying the groundwork for a one world religion ie. Chrislam?

Many changes, many factors come into play each a stone in the foundation of the Antichrist's one-world government and one world religion. Western governments in Europe and North America are openly accepting and subsidizing hundreds of thousands of military aged males from terrorist sponsoring countries to immigrate resulting in increased acts of terrorism throughout their lands. In the United States, Islamic indoctrination has become mandatory in the nation's middle schools. Where the teachers literally walk their students through the steps of becoming Muslim. Muslim prayer rooms are provided for Muslim students, while Christian students are punished for mentioning Jesus or handing out candy canes with a Christian message during the Christmas season. The governmental, bureaucratic hypocrisy is astounding! When Christian parents complain about the Islamic indoctrination of their children their complaints fall

The Great Deception of the Mandela Effect

on deaf ears and they are verbally abused being called racist and islamophobic.

Let's consider the subject of UFOs for a moment. This has been a popular topic for sometime. There are people who believe aliens from space are coming to save us from ourselves, others claim it was aliens in ancient history who created the first humans as an experimentand that aliens are the gods of the ancient world. Truth be told aliens are the watchers, the fallen angels, those that gave up their natural domain to mate with human women. They are the father's of the nephilim and are anything but our benifactors as some will claim.

The mandela Effect, I suspect, is such a deception, I don't doubt that there are those in the world who would implant false memories in the populace as an experiement in mass mind control, or that scientists would experiment in opening portals to other dimensions if they could, but I sincerely doubt that either of those are the underlying cause of the mandela effect. I suspect that the root cause of this phenomena is spiritual in nature and the the objective of this spiritual phenomenon is to cause doubt through cognitive

The Great Deception of the Mandela Effect

disonance within the elect in a final satanic attempt to decieve us into accepting the claims of divinity of the anti-Christ and usher into the world great tribulation before the second coming of Christ.

I advise that we look to strengthen our relationship with Jesus through prayer and trust the Holy Spirit to remind us of all things we learned before bible verses began to change.

John 14:26 Where Christ promises us that the Father will send the Holy Spirit to teach us all things, and bring all things to your remembrance, whatsoever Christ has taught us. This is where I believe we can hope that we will not be deceived and that we can trust in the promptings of the Holy Spirit in guiding us in understanding our bibles.

John 14:26 "But the Comforter, which is the Holy Ghost, whom the Father will send in my name, he shall teach you all things, and bring all things to your remembrance, whatsoever I have said unto you. Peace I leave with you, my

The Great Deception of the Mandela Effect

peace I give unto you: not as the world giveth, give I unto you. Let not your heart be troubled, neither let it be afraid."

What do I get from those passages? Very simply we who have been marked by the Holy Spirit and belong to Christ have been purchased at a great price and can rely on the Holy Spirit to direct us and guide us in these times of great deception.

The Great Deception of the Mandela Effect

Appendix A

Exodus 18:3

3 And her two sons; of which the name of the one was Gershom; for he said, I have been an alien in a strange land:

Exodus 22:7

7 If a man shall deliver unto his neighbour money or stuff to keep, and it be stolen out of the man's house; if the thief be found, let him pay double.

Exodus 34:19

19 All that openeth the matrix is mine; and every firstling among thy cattle, whether ox or sheep, that is male.

Ezekiel 23:17

17 And the Babylonians came to her into the bed of love, and they defiled her with their whoredom, and she was polluted with them, and her mind was alienated from them.

The Great Deception of the Mandela Effect

Ezekiel 23:18

18 So she discovered her whoredoms, and discovered her nakedness: then my mind was alienated from her, like as my mind was alienated from her sister.

Ezekiel 23:22

22 Therefore, O Aholibah, thus saith the Lord God; Behold, I will raise up thy lovers against thee, from whom thy mind is alienated, and I will bring them against thee on every side;

Ezekiel 23:28

28 For thus saith the Lord God; Behold, I will deliver thee into the hand of them whom thou hatest, into the hand of them from whom thy mind is alienated:

5 And I will make Rabbah a stable for camels, and the Ammonites a couching place for flocks: and ye shall know that I am the Lord.

Ezekiel 48:14

The Great Deception of the Mandela Effect

14 And they shall not sell of it, neither exchange, nor alienate the first-fruits of the land: for it is holy unto the Lord.

Matthew 17:21
Matthew 18:11
Matthew 23:14

Mark 9:44
Mark 9:46
Mark 11:26
Mark 15:28

Luke 17:36
Luke 23:17

John 5:4

Acts 8:37
Acts 15:34
Acts 24:7

The Great Deception of the Mandela Effect

Acts 28:29

Romans 16:24

The Great Deception of the Mandela Effect

Appendix B

Isaiah 11:6King James Version (KJV)The wolf also shall dwell with the lamb, and the leopard shall lie down with the kid; and the calf and the young lion and the fatling together; and a little child shall lead them.

Or was it the lion shall lay down with the lamb?

The Great Deception of the Mandela Effect

The shoebill (*Balaeniceps rex*) also known as whalehead or shoe-billed stork, is a very large stork-like bird. Have you ever heard of this bird before? Is it a mandamimal?

The Great Deception of the Mandela Effect

Pteropus, belonging to the megabat suborder, Megachiroptera, are the largest bats in the world. They are commonly known as the fruit bats or flying foxes. The fruit bats I remember are little black bats, not this vulture sized monstrosity. Could it be another mandanimal?

The Great Deception of the Mandela Effect

The Great Deception of the Mandela Effect

Below you see a photograph from a museum exhibit of the Kennedy assassination. Note the number of seats in the car.

THE ASSASSINATION OF PRESIDENT KENNEDY

169

The Great Deception of the Mandela Effect

The Great Deception of the Mandela Effect

Here is a photograph taken from a Life magazine article on JFK's assassination. A photograph taken from the parade moments before JFK is murdered. Note the number of seats in the car. Another photograph, just moments before the assassination. Some people remember four people in the car, others six. This is probably the best example available of residual evidence of the Mandela effect.

The Great Deception of the Mandela Effect

Where do you remember South America to be located? Due south of North America or thousands of miles to the east?

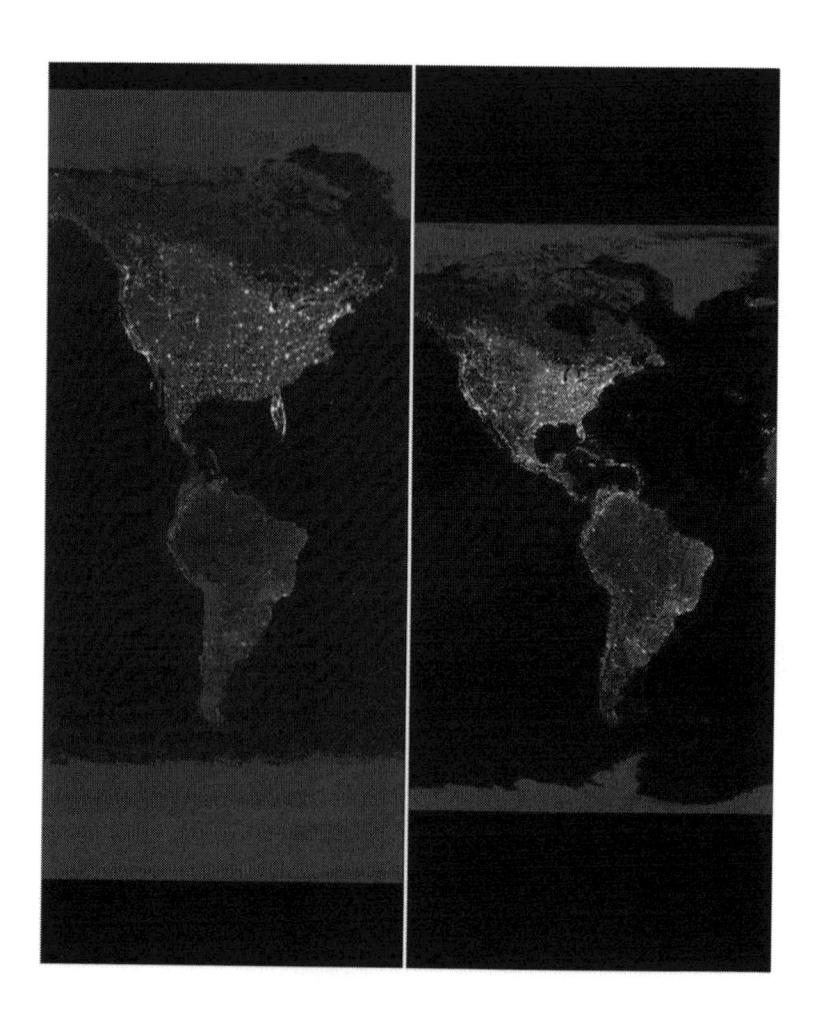

The Great Deception of the Mandela Effect

Also by Lewis Stanek

"A Gathering of Sparrows"
"Angels and Demons, A Biblical Introduction to the Supernatural"
"The Joy of Prayer"
"Hauntings"
"The Haunting of Reuversweerd"
"The Illustrated Secrets of Enoch"
"The Radical Christian"
"The Mandella Effect Study Gospel of Matthew"

The Great Deception of the Mandela Effect

The Great Deception of the Mandela Effect

About the Author

Lewis Stanek was born in Elmhurst, Illinois on March 9th, 1954 at Elmhurst memorial Hospital. He was a sickly child and his earliest memory is of pushing against the wall through the bars of a metal hospital crib and a nurse in a starched white cap pushing the crib back into place. He spent his very early childhood growing up in the western suburbs of Chicago, Illinois. When he turned eighteen he enlisted in the United States Air Force, where after completing his training, he was assigned to the 3rd Combat Communications Group, and stationed at Tinker Air Force Base in Oklahoma City, Oklahoma. Lewis is a Vietnam era veteran. After his discharge from the Air Force he attended the College of Dupage and completed an Associate in Science degree. He then attended Chicago State University earning a Bachelor of Science degree, and much later earned a Master of Religious Studies degree from Nations University.

The Great Deception of the Mandela Effect

Lewis met his wife Mary Diane in August of 1984 and after a whirlwind romance they were married in November of 1985 in a religious ceremony at Antioch Baptist Church in Chicago, Illinois. He is a professed member of the Society of the Cross and a member of the Order of Centurions. He has long held an interest in the supernatural and in writing supernatural horror fiction. Lewis currently lives in Dixon, Illinois with his wife Mary and three of his four children Melissa, Christian, and Zoe. Lewis' eldest son El'Ahrai lives in Illinois with his wife Kathy and their daughter Maggy.

Printed in Great Britain
by Amazon